Barbara Ann
Right Speech,
tfold Path to
id sensitivity,
she offers hundreds of simple, practical teachings designed to make the transformative practice of mindful communication a habit—in the old-fashioned way, through conversation, as well as in the modern world of texting, emails, and social media."

> —**Carol Krucoff, E-RYT**, yoga therapist at Duke Integrative Medicine and author of several books, including *Yoga Sparks*

"*What Would Buddha Say?* provides a fantastic blueprint for speaking to others with kindness, compassion, consideration, and respect. If we all followed Barbara Ann Kipfer's advice, we'd hurt each other less, help each other more, and say fewer things we regret."

> —**Lori Deschene**, founder of tinybuddha.com and author of *Tiny Buddha: Simple Wisdom for Life's Hard Questions* and *Tiny Buddha's Guide to Loving Yourself*

"Kipfer brings us a companion brimming with reminders to speak authentically and from the heart, as if we had a tiny friend in our pocket who occasionally pulled at our sleeve to ask, *What Would Buddha Say?* In these days, when we cannot trust so much of what our eyes show us or the words that reach our ears, her book presses the reset button, reminding us the truth begins first in how we speak to ourselves."

—**Kimber Simpkins**, yoga teacher and author of *Full*

THE *FOLLOWING BUDDHA* SERIES

Based on the teachings of the Eightfold Path, the *Following Buddha* series offers ancient wisdom to help you thrive in the modern world. Designed for both the avid Buddhist and the casual reader alike, these fun and accessible books provide thousands of teachings and affirmations to help you navigate all aspects of life—from building meaningful relationships, to balancing work and home life, to simply choosing one's words wisely.

If you want to act, think, or speak more like Buddha would, the enlightening books in this series will be your go-to guides.

Visit www.newharbinger.com for more books in this series.

What Would Buddha Say?

1,501 RIGHT-SPEECH TEACHINGS

for **COMMUNICATING MINDFULLY**

Barbara Ann Kipfer

New Harbinger Publications, Inc.

Publisher's Note

This publication is designed to provide accurate and authoritative informa-
tion in regard to the subject matter covered. It is sold with the understand-
ing that the publisher is not engaged in rendering psychological, financial,
legal, or other professional services. If expert assistance or counseling is
needed, the services of a competent professional should be sought.

Distributed in Canada by Raincoast Books

Copyright © 2015 by Barbara Ann Kipfer
New Harbinger Publications, Inc.
5674 Shattuck Avenue
Oakland, CA 94609
www.newharbinger.com

Cover design by Amy Shoup; Text design by Michele Waters-Kermes;
Acquired by Melissa Valentine; Edited by Ken Knabb

Library of Congress Cataloging-in-Publication Data on file

Printed in the United States of America

17   16   15

10   9   8   7   6   5   4   3   2   1   First printing

Thank you to New Harbinger for the opportunity to present this material. A big, giant thanks to my editor and husband, Paul Magoulas, who inspires me to practice more Right Speech myself.

There are many inspirations in my life, especially my sons Kyle Kipfer and Keir Magoulas, as well as supportive friends and coworkers. Thank you to everyone.

—Barbara Ann Kipfer

Contents

Foreword   xi

Introduction   1

Teachings   7

Essays   305

Anger ❀ Arguing and Fighting ❀ Asking
for What You Want or Need ❀ Being Present
❀ Bullying ❀ Children ❀ Commenting
and Opinion ❀ Complaining ❀ Conversation
❀ Criticism ❀ Dating ❀ E-mailing
❀ Empathy ❀ Encouragement ❀ Family
❀ Forgiveness ❀ Friends ❀ Getting to
Know Someone ❀ Gratitude and
Appreciation ❀ Humility ❀ Humor
❀ Instructions ❀ Intention ❀ Internal
Talk ❀ Internet ❀ Irritation, Frustration,
Annoyance ❀ Kindness ❀ Listening
❀ Meetings ❀ Neighbors ❀ Overthinking
❀ Patience ❀ Pets ❀ Public Places
❀ Reacting and Responding ❀ Reading
❀ Relatives ❀ Silence and Quiet ❀ Social
Media ❀ Solitude ❀ Strangers ❀ Suffer
ing and Pain ❀ Sympathy ❀ Telephone
Calls ❀ Text Messaging ❀ Thinking
❀ Timing ❀ Truth ❀ Work and Work
Relationships ❀ Writing

Meditations for Right Speech 407

Listening Meditation 1 ❀ Listening
Meditation 2 ❀ Listening Meditation 3
❀ Hearing Meditation ❀ Tone Of Voice
Meditation ❀ Forgiveness Meditations
❀ Compassion Meditation ❀ Meditation
For Changing Negative Thoughts
❀ Meditation For Changing Negative
Mind States

Foreword

When I ponder the question "What would Buddha say?" what first comes to mind isn't words at all, but rather an image. It is an image of a person, seated. The face expresses inner peace and kindness, combined with resolve, strength, and fierce loyalty to depth and directness, where everything extra is stripped away; a face that has experienced great joy and significant difficulty. One hand touches the earth, representing a connection to peace and compassion. The other hand wields a sword—not as a weapon, but representing the ability to cut through obstacles and falsehoods, clearing away the brambles to get to the simple and powerful truth that lives within each of us. Together—the face, a hand touching the earth, and the sword of compassion—they remind and encourage us to speak truthfully, without embellishment, and with the intention to help others.

What will you say? Isn't this the question?

Here Barbara Ann Kipfer serves us a rare meal. She combines a variety of ingredients: words to encourage right speech, essays to guide our speech during everyday life, and meditations on skillful speech meant to support us in finding our grounding. Each course contains words to guide our inner and outer communication. Some of these words are gentle, like a hand touching the ground. Other words have the power to cut through to the core of our being, like a sword.

Words are powerful. One way to view our lives is through our words. Our lives can be seen as one word following another, one sentence after another. Notice how our inner dialogue shapes our outer dialogue. See how our speech shapes our decisions and our actions. Pay attention to how dynamic and changing our lives are—we are—and the need to grow and deepen and align our deepest intentions with what we say.

My scientist colleagues are fond of saying that our brains are story-telling machines, weaving our thoughts, story after story. Through deep listening, we can become more aware and more intimate with these stories, and little by little transform and align our inner and outer speech.

Underlying the practice of right speech is a core teaching of the Buddha—the teaching of impermanence, the fact that everyone and everything changes. Everything—you, others, relationships, and our environment. How does right speech manifest at this time in your life, with the motivations and aspirations you currently experience, with the relationships you have in this chapter of your life? And how can you more deeply connect to your direct experience in order to communicate more authentically?

What stories do you tell yourself? Do you see the world through the lens of doubt and mistrust, or do you notice how love is being communicated? This practice, of noticing love, can reframe and transform how you experience yourself and others. Just this simple practice of noticing. How do you communicate love, with and without words?

Please, take your time with the words in this book. Relax, sit down, have a cup of tea. Let yourself drink in these words. Can you hear each sentence with an open, fresh, and curious mind? These are not just ordinary words. These are words meant to be considered, absorbed, and most of all practiced.

May our words create mutual understanding and love.

—Marc Lesser
CEO, Search Inside Yourself
Leadership Institute

Introduction

Right Speech is one of the elements in Buddha's Eightfold Path to enlightenment. The concept of Right Speech is to refrain from lying, divisive speech, harsh speech, and senseless speech. Practicing Right Speech is a very valuable tool in achieving happiness.

A little reflection will show that speech and the written word can have enormous consequences for good or for harm. Speech can break lives, create enemies, and start wars, or it can give wisdom, heal divisions, and create peace. We can appreciate the need to make our speech more "right." This book was written to offer reminders to make Right Speech a habit, short essays that go into a little more depth about issues and topics involving Right Speech, and a meditations section that focuses on improving listening and positive communication.

We too often express pessimism or criticism that does not need to be voiced. We make comments about what other people say—really just to hear ourselves talk. We don't stop to ask whether we really need to say what we say, or whether what we are about to say is kind or useful. We blurt out opinions that are hurtful, even if they are "honest." And we lie, talk about others when they are not there, exaggerate, put down and diminish people and things, and talk in unnecessary absolutes and superlatives.

For every one of us there is room for improvement in this area. We can train ourselves to speak at the proper time, to speak the truth, to speak gently, to speak beneficially, and to speak from a friendly heart.

You can redefine spiritual life to be your day-to-day life, lived with intention and integrity. Every routine thing, from resolving a conflict to reading a bedtime story, can be part of your spiritual practice. Instead of going through these things on automatic pilot or without care as to what you are saying, you can make daily activities personal and really be there, really pay attention. You can make mindful communication a cornerstone of your spiritual life.

Paying acute attention to each happening, each action, each word is called mindfulness. It's so easy to go on autopilot. You may think autopilot saves you time—but that is simply not true. When you are not "in the moment," you may forget things, bobble things, and do or say unnecessary things that actually cost you time, money, and more.

As you practice mindfulness during everyday activities, you will breathe more deeply and see more wonders. You will likely become more insightful, more content, and maybe more trusting. You will be more kind and thoughtful. Turn to the "Teachings" section, opening to any page, for a quick refresher or reminder to stay on the path of positive communication. Read an essay that examines a part of your life where you would like to see improvement. And just as you hopefully make sure to do regular physical exercise, try to incorporate meditation exercises into your life, which will help you achieve better mental health and poise when speaking, writing, or listening.

Mindfulness of what you speak and write is the focus of this book. If you say what's true for you, and say it clearly and kindly, you get one kind of result. But if you use a sharp tongue, speak falsely, exaggerate, or leave out the parts that are most important to you, you get different results: unnecessary conflicts, lost opportunities, a tightness in your chest, and so on.

The most important person to speak truly to is yourself, with inner speech. Negative inner talk only creates a negative inner emotional landscape. Show as much compassion to yourself as you would toward others and watch your life begin to change for the better.

Minimize the harm you do to others through your speech. Ask yourself what it is like for other people who are subjected to your speech. How would you feel if someone said the same thing to you? Put yourself in the other person's shoes. Maximize the good in your speech as you take steps toward awakening. And then there are the basic precepts: avoid lying, slanderous speech, harsh speech, idle speech, and gossip. Better yet, don't talk if you cannot improve on silence!

Teachings

If you have trouble knowing how to speak, try to imagine what the Buddha would say if he were in your situation.

Develop patience not for pleasure but to cultivate transcendent detachment. Let nothing that comes your way throw you.

Be soft-spoken.

If a relationship has become difficult, it may be because you have nourished your judgment and your anger, not your compassion.

Listening is an art. Listen with a still and concentrated mind. Then it is possible to be responsive to what is being said.

The blow of a whip raises a welt, but a blow of the tongue crushes bones. (Apocrypha, Ecclesiasticus)

Look for the many ways people
   communicate their love without saying it.

When you avoid people who differ from you,
   you shut yourself off from different
   perspectives and reduce your capacity for
   creative solutions.

Your inner stories are based on your own
   opinions. By listening deeply and openly to
   your inner dialogue, you can replace the
   inner authority figure with a more loving,
   nurturing voice.

The more you practice concentrating on the
   breath, the longer you will be able to
   sustain a mindful listener's composure, free
   from internal distraction.

Anger is like picking up hot coals with your
   bare hands and trying to throw them at
   the person you're angry at. Who gets
   burned first?

Avoid using "should" and absolutes like "never," "always," and "every." Absolutes are hot-button words that can easily shut down the other person's willingness to listen.

Poke holes of wakefulness into your mindless communication habits.

What you do not say in a situation is often as important as what you say.

Listening to your words during stressful discussions is essential to avoid fueling the fire.

You can align your speech to the principles of what is truthful and what is most kind and helpful.

Speak only that which you know yourself, see by yourself, and find by yourself.

An alert, calm state of mindfulness, achieved through regular practice, begins to permeate every interaction.

Take the time to express support for someone else's project or work.

Connection is your true nature; you just have to learn to permit it.

The precept of Noble Silence is practiced with no radio, no phone, no television, no writing, no reading, no Internet.

You can stop what you are doing right now and send an e-mail that contains Right Speech.

Remember that how you say something is as important as what you say.

An injury is much sooner forgotten than an insult. (Lord Chesterfield)

Is the nonstop talker an admired person?

Befriending silence is a process of learning
   to befriend yourself.

When you get into a conversation with
   someone, stay away from your own agenda.
   Ask a few open-ended questions that begin
   with "why," "what," or "how" to get the
   other person talking.

When you say something to someone, she
   may not accept it. Do not argue or try to
   explain it intellectually; just listen to her
   until she finds something wrong with her
   own objections.

When in doubt, go for kindness and
   postpone saying anything difficult.

When you live in the present moment, you
   can be aware of your intentions and can
   see their causal relationship with words.

If the point you want to make is sound and well grounded, there is no need for aggression or annoyance.

Speech is one area in which karma can be seen in an easy and direct way.

If you have questions or concerns, place them in the center of the circle for the whole group to contemplate and address.

Meditation siphons off the pools of old collected experience, allowing you to act skillfully and compassionately in the present instead of reacting to the past. Let go, forgive, and accept.

Send an e-mail or leave a voicemail message just to say "I love you."

The Five Precepts of Buddhism are the
foundation for Right Speech: abstain from
taking life, from taking what is not given,
from false speech, from sexual misconduct,
and from taking intoxicants.

When your speech is kindly, people will be
joyful. When it is polite, you will have
many friends.

When you are truthful, you can be relied
upon. When you refrain from slander or
backbiting, you will be trusted.

The way to break the cycle of doing harm
and harm being done to you is to refrain
from blowing up and to convert the angry
energy into a determination to be tolerant
and patient.

You can put an issue in the foreground and
the noise in the background.

It is unrealistic to expect to immediately switch from anger or hate to compassion and love. Patience and tolerance are the middle ground.

Recognize that words are imperfect, so give them limited importance.

A mindful listener is one who allows the speaker to express his heart and mind and expound on his ideas without censure.

Silence remains, inescapably, a form of speech. (Susan Sontag)

Negative speech creates an environment in which it becomes difficult to do anything positive. You cannot feel good about yourself when you intentionally hurt someone else.

You are faced with guilt and remorse when you speak negatively. Why should anyone trust you if you speak harshly?

People carry deep wounds in their hearts that have been inflicted by words of anger.

Be mindful and let your speech come from the heart.

If you get caught in a lie, it will be assumed that it is not the first lie that you told.

We have an equal need to see, hear, and know others for who they are, to celebrate their joy and empathize with their pain.

Sometimes the most skillful speech is Noble Silence.

If you know anything that is helpful and true, find the right time. Think about what you are about to say; make sure that it will be helpful and also true, and the right time has come.

The right time to speak is when the other person is agreeable to listening and is peaceful. It should also be at a time when you have loving feelings for that other person.

Sitting meditation practice trains your mind to slow down and interrupt the speed of your thought process.

Whenever you are about to do or say something, ask yourself if the action or words will result in well-being or harm. If well-being, then do or say it. If harm, then do not do or say it.

Weigh the advantages of forgiveness and resentment. Then choose.

Listen without the imprisoning frame of your imagined and remembered stories, so you can truly communicate with others.

Arrive at a meeting a few minutes early so you have time to relax and breathe mindfully.

Satisfying short-term desires will never make you deeply happy or satisfied with life. Consider the long-term effects of your words and actions.

Do you have the patience to wait till your mud settles and the water is clear? Can you remain unmoving till the right action arises by itself? (Lao-tzu)

Engaging in harsh, abusive, or sarcastic speech keeps others from trusting in or listening to you. The listener will try to protect himself, avoid the abuse, or be equally aggressive.

As you become more conscious, more aware, you discover the joys of listening and let go of your need to control a conversation.

When you are truthful, you will be trusted.

May my words create mutual understanding and love.

Be quiet and let your actions speak for you.

How you speak to yourself can have a powerful effect on what happens in your life.

Next time you talk to your best friend, relish the pauses and also the trust flowing within the conversation.

Lower your voice.

The act of saying something kind, true, and honest is in itself the reward.

If you want others to listen and understand you better, think about what makes you want to listen.

Mindful breathing is the first step to mindful communicating because it relaxes you in body and mind.

Respond with humor.

In any meeting, practice being open and listening to the experience and insight of others.

Make a mental note when you have discovered that wrong speech leads to harm. Tell the person using wrong speech—but only when she is ready to hear it.

Imagine that all your comments and opinions are like drops of water falling into a pond and that the ripples represent the signals you send out to those around you.

Remember that you also communicate through energy, emotions, gestures, eye contact, and facial expressions.

As you connect with yourself, you begin connecting more deeply with other people. Without the first step, the second step is not possible.

Refrain from using speech that is hurtful.

The voice is a second face. (Gerard Bauer)

Undertake for one week not to speak about anyone who is not present.

You can train yourself to speak the truth in such a way that, in the end, the other person can accept it.

When you are trying to control others, what you are typically doing is watching somebody else instead of being mindful of your own actions.

Be open to constructive criticism, and learn even from hostile opinions.

The reason why we have two ears and only one mouth is that we may listen the more and talk the less. (Zeno of Citium)

Close your lips and say something!

Cultivating mindfulness, care, and simplicity in your speech reminds you that you are a part of a whole whose harmony relies on each of the parts living and speaking with kindness and compassion.

When you are frustrated or restless, ask: What am I wanting now? What is wrong with what I have? Welcome what life is offering you in the moment. It is a way to calm your cravings.

Often, when listening to someone who needs your help, the best thing to do is to remain silent and just listen.

Refraining from wrong speech means not only telling the truth but avoiding useless and frivolous talk.

Mindfulness makes it possible to recognize what you are about to say before you say it, and thus offers you the freedom to choose when to speak, what to say, and how to say it.

Regular practice of Right Speech develops integrity, character, and self-respect, and these qualities give speech and even silence a certain power that cannot be measured but is felt.

The purpose of communication is to help yourself and others be more awake to what is true and real.

Act upon the inspirational words you read.

Do you use speech or silence to hide who you are?

The power of silence is that it teaches you to listen. Listening wholeheartedly includes receiving the feeling, emotion, and intention beneath the words.

The first consideration in the act of speaking is the choice to remain silent. If you choose to speak, you should make sure that the words spoken are a benefit for both yourself and others.

Summarizing is a technique that sends the subliminal message, "I am repeating what I think you said, because I really want to understand your viewpoint."

Endeavor to make your speech become much simpler, calmer, and more worthy.

Do what you say and say what you mean.

Do any complaints—even those tempered with humor—serve any purpose? Wouldn't a more direct request or suggestion alleviate a problem?

Open up and listen. Expand your attention to the physical environment. Allow your senses to take in the nonverbal messages from the other people.

Make a confession while you still have the chance.

Once you have encountered how you are feeling and thinking, then you can express yourself honestly and clearly.

Flattery and put-downs are discouraging. There is no use in inflating yourself at the expense of others. Investigate any instance when you compare yourself to others, positively or negatively.

Mindfulness can help make your conversations deeper, more meaningful, more satisfying. It's a combination of mindful speech and deep listening.

In a situation with an obnoxious cell phone user, the best approach may be to move away or politely ask the talker to lower her voice.

You can never really take your words back, so it is critical that you develop such mindfulness about your speech that you do not start rumors or gossip in the first place.

Learning to take care of your speech is learning to take care of your thoughts, feelings, and mind. Learn to cultivate loving-kindness, compassion, wisdom, and simplicity as the seeds from which your speech is born.

Someone may say things that are full of wrong perceptions, bitterness, accusation, and blaming. If you don't practice mindfulness, you will lose your capacity to listen compassionately.

When you are ready to listen deeply, you can listen without interrupting.

The practice of giving someone else your eye contact and your whole focus is a precious gift.

If you are used to having music playing while you work, drive, or exercise, try doing these activities without music. Make space for silence in your life.

If you usually watch television before you sleep, try going without it and sit or lie in silence. At first, the silence may irritate you, but eventually you will calm your mind and change the need to be entertained.

Silence enables you to deeply listen to your environment. This includes the words as well as the subtler, unspoken messages from other people.

Try to keep your mouth shut when you notice you have a strong desire to be right.

It is terrible to speak well and be wrong. (Sophocles)

Value silence.

If you arrive at your workplace having already practiced mindfulness, you'll be happier and more relaxed, and successful communication will come a lot more easily.

When you intend to move or speak, first examine your mind and then act appropriately and with composure.

We become our words.

To widen the gap of time between perceiving a message and interpreting its content is the essence of mindful listening.

You can only control yourself, so take the higher road and speak kindly even to difficult people. Practice patience.

Pay close attention to every word you speak. Respect the power of your own words. If you do this, your words will become increasingly powerful.

Once you have some understanding and insight into your own suffering, you begin to be better at understanding and communicating with others.

Practice stress-reducing communications and active listening.

Train yourself to listen with compassion.

The Buddha taught complete honesty, that everything a person says should be truthful and helpful.

Notice when you are tearing others down. That same critic is also tearing *you* down.

When two partners return home from a day of work, it makes a difference when they create space and time to listen to each other and to ask, "What were the highs and lows of your day?"

Over time in a long-term relationship, our boundaries start to erode. We can restore this by paying attention and not taking each other for granted.

Remember that most of the people you listen to do not use Right Speech.

Take responsibility for what you say.

Let the Buddha speak through you with healing words of acceptance, love, compassion.

Don't become nervous about the absence of speech; allow yourself and others to be silent.

Ask yourself, Am I open to constructive criticism and learning from even hostile opinions?

It is nice to be right, but it is even better to be in touch with the truth, no matter whose mouth it comes from.

It is good to examine impatience and anger when they arise. It helps to listen to the moment, breathe, let things be as they are, and let go into patience.

What is it that you truly wish to say?

Validate what you are hearing by repeating the words back.

Don't get angry with the insults or bad talk of others. If you laugh and ignore attempts to provoke you, people will like you, not dislike you.

What if everyone did their part to work in the direction of Right Speech? What could be overcome by this practice? What would be the outcome on a personal and global level?

High on your list of things to say should be compliments; words of encouragement; expressions of support, appreciation, and love; unambiguous comments and questions; or invitations to do things others like.

Better than a thousand meaningless statements is one meaningful word which, having been heard, brings peace. (Buddha)

Closing the door to honest feedback from others is like cutting the string on a kite. Your mind drifts further from the ground of reality and you are tossed around by the winds of fear. Listen and do not add your own judgment or ideas to what others say.

To listen closely and reply well is the highest perfection we are able to attain in the art of conversation. (La Rochefoucauld)

Mindful communication is the language of your true nature, which has never been damaged by trauma nor limited by your negative ideas about who you are.

Eliminate the meaningless chatter from your communication.

Many of your words have or seem to have no meaning but carry the deeper need to be visible and acknowledged by others.

Loving speech and deep listening are key to community building. Learn to speak in a way that will not cause suffering in yourself and your community.

Use your words to encourage others.

The quieter you become, the more you can hear. (Ram Dass)

Pretend you are talking to the Buddha or Jesus. This will prevent you from gossiping.

Don't notice the tiny flea in the other person's hair and overlook the lumbering yak on your own nose. (Tibetan proverb)

A fool uttereth all his mind. (The Bible)

When you catch yourself yelling at someone, remember the times you have been yelled at and how you felt. This will wake you up and you will find a better way to tell that person what you want to say.

Right Speech is abstaining from lying; it is determining whether the time for speech is appropriate and whether speaking is both useful and truthful; it is speaking in a way that causes no harm.

What is truthful speech? Truthful speech is not overstated, taken out of context, or blown up out of proportion.

Resist the urge to tell others what they need.

Encourage someone's story as you are listening to it by rewording it with positive words.

One reason we have trouble communicating with others is that we do so when we are angry. We believe that we are angry because of something others did and we want them to know it.

Anger distorts the truth when you believe you are good and the other person is bad. You can't see any good qualities in another person when you're angry with him.

Be quiet for a moment, until the right words arise by themselves.

If you follow Right Speech precepts, you will find yourself talking less and saying more. Your chatter will stop and the quality of your conversation will improve.

You can start by doing everything possible to avoid the people who wish you harm, in order to keep them from being able to carry out any hurtful plans.

Become aware of when your mind is judging. If you acknowledge it without giving it open, clear attention, the judging mind begins to dissolve itself.

You can be mindful of what you are doing when you speak—of what the motivation is and how you are feeling. You can also be mindful of listening.

Many of us suffer because our communication with other people is difficult. At work, for example, we often feel we have tried everything and there is no way to reach our colleagues.

Being silent is better than speech that is not true or useful.

By maintaining silence, you can be more fully aware of such things as how quickly you eat, how well you chew your food, what food you desire, and how much you eat.

Your words and thoughts constantly distract you from what you intuit. Your mind then creates a distorted view of reality that you take to be true.

Speak gently to everyone and they will respond accordingly.

If you learn to tolerate suffering without taking offense at it or taking it personally, then you are fortified against whatever anger can do to you. Anger cannot make you blow up.

Kindness and compassion do not always mean that we say yes.

Spend as long as necessary listening to someone talk about what's troubling her.

When asked a question, pause up to sixty seconds before answering. It is likely that the answer will include reflection, examination of intention, preview of tone—and be a wiser response.

Why do we talk so much? Talking hides loneliness, boredom, fear, emptiness. But it also blocks our heart. We can grow only when things get quieter and we really see.

See if you can simply listen without interrupting. Can you listen without judging or even reacting to what is being said?

There are two keys to effective and true communication. The first is deep listening. The second is loving speech.

Watch every act and every thought. Watch every desire. Watch even the small gestures: walking, talking, eating, taking a shower. When you watch, clarity arises.

The more watchful you become, the more you slow down and become graceful. Your chattering mind becomes quiet.

Habitual language that produces angry "seeds" eventually results in an angry person.

Sensitivity and discernment are essential to Right Speech.

Awareness and mindfulness sometimes buckle under the weight and force of your feelings, thoughts, and words.

You can speak well if your tongue can deliver the message of your heart. (John Ford)

Be generous, offer compliments, give accurate feedback, listen carefully.

All human beings are gifted with a natural wakefulness that makes us question our own opinions. This positive kind of doubt is like a good friend who asks, Why are you saying this?

If you have a strong habit involving talking that is not serving you well, you can make a conscious practice of restraint in that area.

When you refrain from harsh speech and gossip, you begin to notice more subtle forms of aggression, such as how you silence people when they say what you don't want to hear.

Your knee-jerk reaction may be to shout or be unkind, but ultimately this is an exhausting, vicious cycle of conflict that has no positive outcome.

The essence of morality and virtue is represented by the wisdom of not harming others, even with words.

Listen for things you have in common with other people, rather than scanning for the ways you are better or worse.

When you leave home in the morning, go with a committed intention to speak only what is truthful, helpful, and sensitive.

By cultivating a voice rooted in wisdom and simplicity, you learn to restrain speech that is harsh or abusive and to cultivate kindness, sensitivity, and respect in your words.

Don't interrupt others.

There's no place where deep listening and loving speech are inappropriate.

Argument seldom convinces anyone contrary to his inclinations. (Thomas Fuller)

Kind words are usually easy to speak.

Remember that take-it-or-leave-it
   information, like giving someone a free tip
   or mentioning a contact that might be of
   interest to him or her, is positive.

Even if yesterday you produced a thought of
   anger and hate, today you can produce a
   thought in the opposite direction, a
   thought of compassion and tolerance.

Using right communication today can help
   us heal the past, enjoy the present, and
   prepare the ground for a good future.

Speak positively and your thoughts will
   follow suit.

Respond to happiness with celebration.

Undertake the training precept of refraining
   from false speech, harmful speech, gossip,
   and slander.

Listen for the quietest sound.

If you are compassionate with yourself, you'll more likely be compassionate toward others.

Do you hear yourself gossiping or criticizing or berating others? You may be doing this to make yourself look better, but instead you put yourself in a negative light.

When you can see the suffering in others, you begin to understand that there is a reason they suffer. You are no longer angry with them. Compassion will arise in your heart.

When compassion is born, you are more peaceful, your mind is clearer, and you will be motivated to say or do something to help others transform their difficulties.

Watch your thoughts; they become your words.

If you think the truth is too shocking, you can find a skillful and loving way to tell it.

When you are angry with someone, you may think you are seeing her clearly. In reality, anger makes you see the person or situation through distorted lenses.

Listen while you are speaking. The mind is quick enough to revise a planned statement on the fly. Hear your tone of voice, the words you choose. Remember that you are having an effect on others.

Drop aggression and defensiveness and face your fears, open your heart. Meditation will teach you how every moment becomes an opportunity to practice.

The first element of Right Speech is to tell the truth.

The mind should be filled with righteous talk: talk that uplifts, talk that helps, talk that soothes.

If you could hear your words and comments through the ears of your listeners, you would be appalled at overgeneralizations, inaccuracies, and insensitive comments you sometimes make.

With the law of karma, you have a choice in each new moment of what response your heart and mind bring to a situation.

Keep your words gentle, loving, accurate, and positive.

In finding the willingness to pause and listen to yourself before you speak, you may discover the confidence and calmness to speak with firmness and clarity.

The next time you want to comment without a true purpose, take a deep breath and think about your motivation. Are your words coming from a judging mind, and aimed at building yourself up?

Before real anger occurs, there is a mental discomfort and an awareness that something is happening that you do not want. By being mindful and aware of that momentary gap before reacting takes over, you can enter into a controlled, graceful response.

The thought manifests as the word; the word manifests as the deed. The deed develops into habit, and habit hardens into character. So watch each thought with care, and let it spring from love.

Saying "I am here for you" is the best gift you can give a loved one. Nothing is more precious than your presence.

Do not throw insults back or get angry with the insults or bad talk of others. Laugh and ignore attempts to provoke you.

If someone is expressing anger toward you, watch your breath and keep it slow and steady. Pause for several seconds and wait. The person may sense that you are giving the go-ahead to get to the heart of the problem.

Is what you want to say an improvement over maintaining silence?

Have the grace to refrain from an unkind word.

Tell the truth. Don't lie or turn the truth upside down. Don't exaggerate. Be consistent. Use peaceful language. Don't use insulting or violent words, cruel speech, verbal abuse, or condemnation.

When someone is needing to talk, be generous, listen carefully, offer compliments, and give accurate feedback.

Being silently attentive is helpful while listening to upset children. If your child comes home complaining about something, don't be tempted to try to talk him out of his feelings.

If you can put your "shoulds," interrogation, and advice aside and instead remain silently attentive to an upset child, the child will feel safe about revealing her emotions.

Give every man thine ear, but few thy voice. (Shakespeare)

The practice of self-reflection takes advantage of the fact that imaginary or remembered stories can arouse emotions just as if they were happening in real-life present time.

Say the sentimental grateful things that you feel but are often too scared to speak aloud.

I cannot speak well enough to be unintelligible. (Jane Austen)

Unrequested advice frequently takes on a preachy tone, even if it is good, sound, and well-meaning.

Have you ever said anything you later deeply regretted?

When you really are sure you have something true and beneficial to say—use compassion. Compassion helps you because compassion is all about the other person, not you.

Imagine never knowingly speaking a lie. Speaking the truth is at the heart of insight meditation practice.

Because speech is so predominant in our lives, and because our words are so consequential, learning the art of skillful communication is a significant aspect of spiritual practice.

Speaking from the heart starts with inner listening.

Mindful listening under stress begins inside and works outward.

Your words can express the values you care about—and in a way that can be heard by others.

Give yourself a couple of hours to write a letter using loving speech.

There are always different ways to express yourself.

Right Speech requires training and practice.

Well-timed silence hath more eloquence than speech. (Martin Farquhar Tupper)

Silence is an excellent way to quiet our habitual busy bodies and overactive rational minds while becoming more receptive, self-reflective, and sensitive.

Whether outright lying, exaggerating, or minimizing, a lie will always be a lie. Speaking should be truthful, useful, and appropriate while causing no harm.

Well-spoken words bear fruit in one who puts them into practice.

Considering all the many ways that communication is integral to your daily life, you see that you can make Right Speech your whole spiritual practice.

Is your listening focused and concentrated in order for you to use the knowledge base you have acquired to examine the validity of the evidence?

See conflict in a positive light in which neither side loses and a new dance is created.

Keep the radio or music off while driving. Each time you stop at a stoplight, stop sign, or in traffic, check your awareness level. Be mindful.

As the listener, it doesn't matter if you cannot offer the solution to the problem. You can be the sounding board, which is frequently all it takes for the speaker to determine her own solution.

When communication is strained, speaking gently can help you meet the challenge of aggression with patience and emotional maturity. You can allow your friend to feel respected even if you disagree with what he is saying.

When you stop talking and thinking and listen mindfully to yourself, one thing you will notice is your greater capacity and opportunities for joy.

Silence, a form of inner fasting, is a time-honored way of hearing your own truth.

Even your smallest, least significant thought, word, or action has real consequences throughout the universe.

The truth is a solid base for a long-lasting relationship. If you don't build your relationship on the truth, sooner or later it will crumble.

What is beneficial speech? It is speech that helps things get better, not worse—even if it takes a while.

Get out of the got-to-tell-all, lay-it-on-the-line syndrome.

If you react to the knowledge that someone is speaking badly of you with a feeling of hurt or anger, then you yourself destroy your own peace of mind.

Strive to be clear that it is the right time to say something and that it is likely to be beneficial.

Before you say something, ask yourself whether your words will build or harm the relationship.

Have you ever told people you were fine even when you felt depressed and sad?

Give yourself the gift of silence. Listen to the silence. Then your feelings and thoughts have a space to live in for a while.

When you have compassion for yourself, you can more easily understand the suffering of others. Your communication will be based on the desire to understand rather than the desire to prove yourself right or make yourself feel better.

Pause and allow silence to be a part of your communication.

In order to see, listen; in order to hear, look.

Men of few words are the best men. (Shakespeare)

If you are angry at a person, that person is not the problem. Your anger is the problem. No matter how much you think the anger is coming from the other person, it is not.

Try to see complaints as coming from a concerned individual who wants things to go smoother between you.

For one day, resolve to let go of judgments and conclusions. Recognize when your point of view is not resting on an actual experience but is simply an opinion.

Find the blessing of inner silence and peace. Teach yourself the amazing tool of being able to just let things go, avoiding the grip of angry, passionate, worried, or depressed thoughts.

It helps to speak with compassion; you are better able to manage your own thoughts and impulses and to contend with the thoughts and impulses of the person you are talking to.

Listen with a sense of humility.

Let your words be straight, simple, and said with a smile. You are what you say.

Your goal in becoming a mindful listener is to quiet the internal noise to allow the whole message and the messenger to be understood.

You can learn a lot about what is really going on in the pause between feeling angry and taking action.

Walk into a situation and be open to whatever arises. If fear arises, instead of reacting to it, respond, "Ah, fear." Allow it space in your mind. Fear then has less impact and you can handle the situation with more confidence.

With Right Speech, people can make suggestions or observations in such a way that the other person can hear and use those things without feeling diminished.

Lying takes three forms—outright lying, exaggerating, or minimizing. It is based on self-centered fear.

If a person speaks with an impure mind, suffering follows. If a person speaks with a pure mind, joy follows.

It does not matter what anyone else says about you because you cannot control what anyone else says. The only thing you can control is your reaction to what is said.

Take a few days to carefully notice the intentions that motivate your speech. Direct your attention to the state of mind that precedes talking, the motivation for your comments, responses you get, and your observations. Try to observe without any judgment.

Try to be particularly aware of whether your speech is even subtly motivated by boredom, concern, irritation, loneliness, compassion, fear, love, competitiveness, greed, hate, and so on.

Be aware of the general mood or state of your heart and mind and how it may be influencing your speech. Notice the motivations in the mind and the speech that flows from them.

Ask yourself: Are my communications healing, harmonizing, and sensitive?

The key to your peace of mind lies not in your circumstances, but in how you respond to them. Life is painful; suffering is optional.

People living in a constant state of irritation or rage are at risk for high blood pressure, strokes, and heart attacks and are prone to arthritis from inflammation of the joints.

Telling tales or making unkind jokes only distances you from others.

Often, by being better listeners ourselves, we can accomplish much more than by trying to change others.

There is nothing weak about not confronting someone directly or aggressively. It is simply a different way of relating to others and helps you to avoid being a victim or an aggressor.

People who honestly mean to be true really contradict themselves much more rarely than those who try to be consistent. (Oliver Wendell Holmes, Sr.)

Compassion looks into the other person (the listener) and feels whether the time is right for that person to hear your truth.

Get into the habit of talking in a meaningful and loving way. You will gradually develop inner qualities that give your words power, allowing them to influence and benefit others.

If you are not able to speak calmly, then do not speak that day. Open your mouth and speak only when you are sure you can use calm and loving speech.

Make the effort to thank someone each day.

For a job interview or public speech: Visualize yourself walking in and exuding self-confidence. You are very relaxed and talking freely and confidently with the interviewer or the audience.

Take a deep breath and tell the truth.

While listening, don't fidget.

We have all spoken rashly and regretted it, and we have all been on the receiving end of angry or hurtful words and have felt their impact.

Most of us have encountered someone who listened to us with such understanding that we felt better just from talking.

You can think about communication in terms of nourishment and consumption. For example, the Internet is an item of consumption, healing but also toxic. Be conscious of what you are reading and watching; make sure that it nourishes you.

If you've spent the time getting to work breathing mindfully and being in the present moment, you will arrive with a clear mind and you'll be able to greet people with a warm and open smile.

Accept criticism, study it, then let it go.

Gossiping is often the communication of your judgments, self-righteousness, and opinions. It is how you define yourself to others and separate good from bad.

Undertake a life of conscious conduct: not killing, not stealing, refraining from sexual misconduct, not using intoxicants heedlessly, and not speaking falsely.

Mindfulness with compassion means you listen with only one intention—to help the other person suffer less.

If you know someone who speaks truthfully and honestly—you realize that this is wonderful, though it can also be painful. It is much better for speech to be true and helpful.

In that moment when story and judgment do not interfere, you discover the rich silence of listening.

During a meeting, practice using loving speech and deep listening. Follow your breathing as you listen. Let one person speak at a time, without interruption.

We wonder how we can uproot the confusion that starts an argument, or get rid of anger or restlessness. Just acknowledge the state of mind by naming it and giving it space. Shine the light of awareness on it and it loses its power.

Use your words to convey patience.

Think of a child hearing her parents fighting. Even if the words are not directed at her, the effect of the angry speech is much the same.

Make your intentions, mind, speech, and thoughts move in harmony with one another.

We use so many words every day and in so many ways. We use them to speak to others and we also use words to speak to ourselves—the incessant internal monologue.

You say something to one person, but when speaking about the same matter to another person you say something different as a way of gaining some advantage. This can cause a lot of suffering on both sides and might even create enemies.

Nothing in a conflict matters enough to merit the suffering you could inflict on yourself and others.

Many people would be more truthful were it not for their uncontrollable desire to talk. (Edgar Watson Howe)

Give advice only when asked—and keep it short!

Speech is a vehicle of love, communion, and awakening.

By training yourself to stop when communication shuts down, you can bring loving attention to the misunderstandings and fears that trigger defensive reactions.

Throughout your life, you are deafened by the voices that exhort you to compete, achieve, possess, and judge.

Practice expressing your appreciation to the people you care about and apologizing right away when you do or say something that hurts them. You can also politely let others know when you have been hurt.

Express gladness in tangible ways.

Treasuring simplicity, healing, and awareness, you learn to refrain from gossip.

Dealing with the unexpected is an opportunity to practice patience and nonaggression.

Silence is a natural mindfulness practice. It is a refuge and a teacher.

Just as you carefully watch your footing on a steep and rocky path, you should speak with the same care to avoid injury or costly mistakes.

Use the power of words to build deeper connections. The connections you make with others, superficial and profound, most often begin with the spoken or written word.

Wise speech is a blend of cultivation and restraint. Cultivate speech that is truthful, helpful, kind, and that leads to harmony or healing.

The five characteristics of well-spoken words are as follows: spoken at the proper time, spoken in line with the truth, spoken beneficially, spoken gently, and spoken with a friendly heart.

Putting aside your agenda and taking the spotlight off yourself is exactly what you need to do when listening under stress. In a calm state, you can set aside your barriers and other defenses and more directly address the issue.

If you could hear yourself as others do, you might be able to understand why you experience some problems at work, at home, and with your friends.

How about refraining from saying anything about anyone who is not present? How about no talking about people who annoy you or those who excite you?

How about no analyzing or dissecting anyone else's behavior or problems—good or bad—unless the person is actually there?

When you stop talking about others, you discover how much time and energy you waste daily on conversations that serve no constructive purpose and take you away from the present moment.

When you are tempted to use words as weapons, ask yourself what you hope to gain.

Simply wanting to say something isn't a reason to say it.

Man does not live by words alone, despite the fact that sometimes he has to eat them. (Adlai Stevenson)

To exaggerate is to weaken. (Jean-François de La Harpe)

Once you can communicate with yourself truthfully, you'll be able to communicate outwardly with more clarity.

A remarkable number of conflicts are easily resolved just by articulating the problem more clearly.

Our society is built on communication: our culture, our systems, our friendships, our love—the whole world around us.

Speak kindly to strangers.

If you sense a story about to start in your mind, say to it and to yourself, Not now. Take a vow not to tell yourself stories.

Everything said can be recalled, if taken back sincerely.

Pause before and after you speak. Pause even as you are speaking to reconnect with your feelings. Pause after another is done speaking, allowing space for what was said to settle.

While sharing your thoughts may be important at times, when you attach to them and are sure you are right, you invite conflict. You try to convince; you do not listen.

See being right as less important, as not providing real satisfaction. See being wrong as not devastating and as something that will pass.

Allow yourself and others to be silent.

When we talk too fast or too slowly, no one understands us.

Words born of silence are words of peace and meaning, compassion and care.

Use thoughts and words of love since everything you think and speak comes back to you.

You are what you do, not only what you do with your body, but also what you do with your words and your mind. Karma is the triple action of your thoughts, your speech, and your bodily actions.

When in doubt as to what to say, remember: it is difficult to put your foot in your mouth when your mouth is closed.

By training yourself in mindfulness, you can learn to genuinely accept yourself as you are—and others as they are—while at the same time responding skillfully to the challenges that block communication.

Learning how to return to the present moment with mindfulness is like a safety net when you are provoked by anger or hatred.

The master directs his straying thoughts. By ruling them, he finds happiness.

Find the words that lead toward happiness, earn the trust and respect of others, and foster loving-kindness.

Use words to help, not harm. Right Speech reminds you to refrain from causing trouble with words that are hurtful or unnecessarily disruptive.

Remind yourself every day to use words that express nondiscrimination, forgiveness, understanding, support, and love.

Very seldom is a liar believed, even when she speaks the truth.

We often think positive things about people, but don't often let them know it.

One never repents of having spoken too little, but often of having spoken too much. (Philippe de Commynes)

Be specific and direct about what you want to communicate.

The second part of Right Speech is to refrain from inventing and exaggerating.

Leave the talking to others.

Encourage a speaker to speak from his heart and expound on his ideas without censure.

Aim to be perfectly truthful, affectionate, helpful, and to promote concord, harmony, unity.

To every thing there is a season, and a time to every purpose under the heaven:...a time to keep silence, and a time to speak... (Ecclesiastes)

If you communicate well in your work environment, not only do you enjoy yourself more, but you create a harmonious atmosphere that will carry over into your work.

Peace is not only the absence of conflict; it also encourages dialogue to solve conflicts in a spirit of mutual understanding and cooperation.

When the mind is soft and nongrasping, your speech becomes soft and nongrasping and you don't get caught in the melodramas that cause pain to yourself and others.

When you like someone, tell him.

Many a time the thing left silent makes for happiness. (Pindar)

Do you practice the teachings of a spiritual life, keep them in your mind, practice them in your speech, and ponder them in your heart?

Speak and act wisely. Know that every action of body, speech, and mind has consequences, a corresponding result. Deep listening and moderation is your mantra in this situation.

Are you ingesting things that grow your understanding and compassion?

A good listener is easy to spot—she is usually someone we look forward to talking with and being around.

A good listener makes the speaker feel valued by encouraging her to expand on her ideas and feelings.

What is well-intended speech? It comes from good will, not ill will; it is constructive and aimed to build up, not tear down.

Though you may not outright lie, there are times when you find yourself compromising and shading the truth. You say things that others want to hear or that you want to hear and believe.

If people in your workplace are open to having a bell sound before a meeting begins, that sound can help everyone come back to their breathing and find some calm.

Before you speak, remind yourself to express dignity and respect.

When you wake up in the morning and before you go to bed, turn off or keep off as much technology as possible. Take care with what you put in your mind at these times.

Write a love letter to each member of your family.

Thank someone for believing in you.

True inner silence puts you in touch with the deeper dimension of being and knowing, awareness and wisdom.

There are times when you are startled or shocked at your words. In listening to yourself, do you sometimes hear your mother or father or the voice of a stranger?

Listen to your tone of voice and recognize that in speaking to another you are touching her heart—and this requires wholehearted attention.

How much attention do you pay to your speech? Do you bring some wisdom and sensitivity to your speaking? What is behind your speech—what motivates it?

Unconditional friendliness comprises the qualities of openness, trust, and accommodation. This is making friends with yourself.

A voice rooted in wisdom treasures truthfulness, respect, and compassion and it honors our interconnectedness.

Less than a minute can make all the difference between open, honest communication and feeling rushed and treated impersonally.

Be swift to hear, slow to speak.

What is conceived well is expressed clearly, /
   And the words to say it with arrive with
   ease. (Nicolas Boileau)

Awareness in your speech is a commitment
   to speaking the truth and to the context
   in which it is spoken. If the timing is
   wrong, then what you say may come across
   as criticism or judgment.

Try to let go of your fears and projections
   and see the simple truth of each moment.
   Understanding and wise responsiveness
   will manifest in your speech, actions, and
   choices.

Are you engaged in a "two-way street"
   conversation or do you shut down the
   traffic with a one-way broadcast?

There can be a domino effect that your angry words trigger. If you look closely, you may notice that your intention isn't to communicate at all, but rather to punish your listener.

Before you speak, contemplate: I am mindful of what I am doing, how I am feeling, and what my motivation is. I talk only when necessary.

Straightforwardness, without the rules of propriety, becomes rudeness. (Confucius)

Remember that it is better not to speak of things you do not understand. (Lao-tzu)

Refrain from useless idle speech and speak words that are meaningful and clear.

Complain less and listen more.

Practice listening for the silences between sounds and noticing the space between thoughts. This foundation allows you to enhance intuition and expand the range of your senses.

Refuse to lie, gossip, or inflame people.

When you lose your focus of attention and the ability to consciously choose what to do or say, mentally stop. Smile to yourself. Chide yourself gently. Then breathe.

If language be not in accordance with the truth of things, affairs cannot be carried on to success. (Confucius)

The Sanskrit word *karma* means "action," and it refers not just to bodily action but to what you express with your body, your words, and your thoughts and intentions.

To listen well, you have to learn to be more empty, to set aside the complexity of your expectations, opinions, and chatter, and the agitation that clouds your mind.

Wrong speech is mainly false speech, gossip, or commenting. Take a vow not to speak about any person not present, even if it is a favorable comment.

Speak and act with loving-kindness.

Look wise, say nothing, and grunt. Speech was given to conceal thought. (Sir William Osler)

Real gentleness comes from knowing that you need to protect your sense of connectedness rather than putting up barriers around your personal territory.

We every day and every hour say things of
   another that we might more properly say of
   ourselves, could we but apply our
   observations to our own concerns.
   (Montaigne)

Keep the listener in mind when speaking.

We do not always use words to communicate
   from our hearts—and then we expect
   others to be mind readers.

When you are at your most agitated, the
   pressure of inner unrest seems to unlock
   your mouth, as if saying your every thought
   were the only way to reclaim inner calm.

Determine to speak truthfully, with words
   that inspire self-confidence, joy, and hope.

Even without speaking, people who feel angry often create an agitated atmosphere; family members who pick up on sighs and gestures grow tense and fearful of conflict.

When your mind is agitated, your harmful thoughts repeat imagined experiences that build emotional reactions.

Know when to bite your tongue.

How often do you discount or reject another's perception of a situation? "It can't be that bad" and "You're making too much fuss about this" are perfect examples of subtle denial.

Apologize immediately if you were thoughtless or cruel, as soon as you recognize your lack of skill and mindfulness.

Inner solitude and Noble Silence give you ways to empty, cleanse, heal, and renew the heart and mind.

Why be unhappy about something if you can do something about it? If you can't do something about it, why be unhappy about it? In fact, why be unhappy about anything *ever*?

Imagine never having to regret anything you say!

A mindful listener asks questions to better understand the speaker and his views.

Lead us toward a speech, which is as beautiful as silence, and toward a silence, which is as beautiful as the sweetest and truest of words. (Jean-Yves Leloup)

If you feel compassion while listening, anger and irritation cannot arise. Learn to listen with only one purpose: to allow the other person to express herself and find relief from her suffering.

Little said is soon amended. (Cervantes)

It is only when you block the spontaneity of listening by focusing on outcome rather than process that listening becomes stilted.

Succeed in not raising your voice during a fight.

Speak and act with a pure mind. When you do, happiness follows.

Giving attention is one of the purest expressions of love. When you give another the gift of listening with your whole heart, separation dissolves and hurt is healed.

If you make a mistake or a bad decision, you can simply acknowledge it, learn what you can from it, resolve to avoid repeating it, and put it aside.

Right Speech does not mean not talking about social problems, political issues, and so on. And it does not mean being passive. It's just being mindful and speaking with a compassionate mind and heart.

Let words come more directly from your heart and not from autopilot. You should not assume you will see a particular person again, so you should exercise care.

When speaking, make sure you say something, preferably something positive and thoughtful.

You should never underestimate the power of your speech.

Let silence empower you.

The core fear of the false self is the feeling of being cut off, unwelcome, depressed. Meet this fear and self-doubt with wakeful kindness.

What if you stop what you are doing and put all your attention on the other person? What if you focus on the other person and not on your own agenda or the next activity of your life?

Listening can be a compassionate, loving form of Right Speech.

In your conversations, you can be so intent on getting your message across that you are not really paying attention to what others say. You are waiting for them to stop speaking so you can talk.

Whether alone or with a friend, you need to create space to deeply listen.

During an argument, when you feel the urge to go for a walk, you are following a healthy instinct to back away before you say or do something to harm your relationship.

Staying connected to others, even to your enemies, is a more successful strategy than hiding behind an imaginary barrier and going it alone.

The art of conversation is the art of hearing as well as of being heard. (William Hazlitt)

Praise doesn't add anything to your qualities or achievements. So let it go.

If the criticism is true, then it's helpful feedback that you can use. If it's not true, then it is only a projection from the other person, and means nothing.

Telling lies arises from an inability or unwillingness to see the situation as it is. To actively practice not lying to yourself and others is liberating.

Unless you are sinless, do not talk about the sins of others.

In the midst of speaking, working, cleaning, or any other activity, stop for a moment. Actively take your attention from the external world and focus it on your breath.

To tell a falsehood is like the cut of a saber; for though the wound may heal, the scar of it will remain. (Gulistan of Sa'di)

Pay attention; it pays off. Stay conscious of what you say and think. Mindfulness keeps negative tendencies in check.

Ask yourself: What matters most at this moment? What do I really care about more than anything at this point? Do I care more about being right or being happy?

Resist telling people how something should be done.

Keeping eye contact and not interrupting shows your respect.

How can you make sure your speech is worthwhile, and not just blather? Without a bit of silence woven into the conversation, there is no time to think, to hear, or to connect.

Continuous chatter blocks out reflective thinking, and it wears out both the speaker and the listener. Some silence invites listening, thoughtful speech, and absorption of what is said.

A basic spiritual practice is to set your intention to be present, honest, and kind in relating to others. Remind yourself of this at the start of the day and before any interaction with others.

Through awareness practice, you can develop a patient and tolerant inner fortitude. This helps you transcend ego reactivity that makes you lash out with words.

Idle speech is meaningless speech used to fill in gaps when you are afraid of silence. It is speech that has no purpose.

It is beautiful and peaceful to stay in a place of silence of mind. Discover the blessing of inner silence and peace.

Start sentences with "I feel." You stop, look within, and identify what you are feeling at that moment. It requires patience and slows or stops what could become a disagreement.

Become aware of your breathing and of what feelings or thoughts are passing through you. Just by doing that, you may calm down and the urge to speak mindlessly may pass.

It's not just what you say—it's how, when, and why you say it.

Know when to keep silent; know when to speak up.

How much of the information you absorb is news and how much is opinion? This is the question you should ask yourself when you are practicing mindful speech.

Keeping your ego out of the spotlight when giving requested advice creates admiration and a willingness to follow through, because the needs of your speakers are taken into consideration.

If you speak harshly to another, you lose your spiritual footing and create pain, causing the other's mind to become disturbed and upset. Keep your words gentle, loving, accurate, and positive.

If you can learn to not be angry with someone who is verbally attacking you, you will arm yourself with tolerance, which is the greatest possible protection.

There is a difference between the raw, unavoidable distresses of life—primary experiences—and the unnecessary suffering created by mindless reactions.

All that we are is the result of what we have thought. If a man speaks or acts with an evil thought, pain follows him. If a man speaks or acts with a pure thought, happiness follows him, like a shadow that never leaves him. (Buddha)

Do you wish people to believe good of you? Don't speak. (Pascal)

In finding your voice, you release the countless voices you have inherited that came with their own values and expectations.

Even a fool, when he holdeth his peace, is counted wise. (The Bible)

Talk about ideals, not people or things.

Eliminate any negative tone from your speech.

Recognize a thought's inherent emptiness. It will dissolve without a trace, like a bird flying through the sky.

You can object to wrong speech by not listening to abusive radio, not watching abusive television, and not buying things with aggressive printed messages.

Take some time to quietly be with a person in pain. Look directly at the other person with warmth. Stay with this process until you develop more compassion for that person.

Gentleness gives you the power to absorb insults and blame and even to say "I'm sorry" when it is really the other person who has caused harm.

It takes remarkable patience and compassion to find the willingness to pause before words of anger are hurled at another.

In the grip of anger, you are no longer the master of your thoughts, speech, and actions. Why choose to be angry if you can stay in control of your feelings and act skillfully?

It doesn't cost anything to have loving speech. (Vietnamese saying)

Allow yourself to question the validity of your opinions and emotional reactions.

The noise in your mind prevents you from taking positive steps toward a successful resolution of a problem and focusing on the issue.

Ask yourself if what you are about to say will be harmful. If your answer is yes, don't say it. Applying meditation in action ensures that your mind is in gear and nobody gets hurt.

The wisest among us have the least to say.

Offer a healing touch, a healing word.

The value of your life depends on the quality of your thinking, speech, and actions.

You can take responsibility for what you say more easily if you are not rushing.

If your heart is large with understanding and compassion, a word or deed will not have the power to make you suffer.

Whenever anger and hatred are involved, they always emerge the winner. The only way out of this vicious cycle is to recognize that the real enemy is anger itself.

Speech is very powerful—and when it is truthful, honest, genuine, and beneficial, it builds harmony with others in society, at work, and with friends, family, and acquaintances.

In human intercourse the tragedy begins, not when there is misunderstanding about words, but when silence is not understood. (Henry David Thoreau)

Silence is sometimes the best answer.

It is a rare person who understands what it is to speak wisely, who is at ease with silence, and who finds equal joy in solitude and in company.

Listening means attending to physical sensations as well as to the voice, facial expressions, gestures, pauses, underlying meanings, and rich nuances that accompany others' spoken words.

Being mindfully present with a friend when communication shuts down is like stepping into the role of a loving parent with a child who's having a nightmare.

How can you quarrel, knowing that life is as fleeting as a rainbow, a flash of lightning, a star at dawn?

If you think twice before you speak, you will find that the majority of the time you will have no occasion to say a word.

Forgiveness is not about punitive justice, but it is an essential component of restorative justice, justice that aims to restore the social balance that the wrongdoing has disturbed.

Before you actually speak, focus on why you want to speak and what you want to say. Get in touch with what is going on within. If you see a negative motivation, don't talk.

When you tell the truth, sometimes the result isn't what you wanted. Tell the truth in such a way that others don't feel threatened, so they can listen.

Rather than habitually giving responses such as "I'm fine" or "I don't know," you must look into your heart and respond with authenticity.

No glass renders a man's form or likeness so true as his speech. (Ben Jonson)

Words have the power to destroy or heal.
When words are both true and kind, they
can change the world.

Talking is like playing the harp; there is as
much in laying the hand on the strings to
stop their vibrations as in twanging them
to bring out their music. (Oliver Wendell
Holmes, Sr.)

If it is false, harmful, and nasty, do not say
it. If it is false, harmful, and pleasant, do
not say it. If it is true, harmful, and nasty,
do not say it. If it is true, helpful, and
pleasant, know when to say it.

Respond to pain with compassion.

The most important step in developing
skillful speech is to think before speaking
or writing.

When you hear yourself using malicious speech, see if you can stop, breathe, and reflect. Hold your tongue for three breaths. If you restrain the impulse often enough, the desire to speak maliciously will come up less frequently.

Speech is often our ignorance made manifest. It is the most common way in which we harm others.

Compassion opens you up to accept your failings and those of others. With that acceptance comes patience, the ability to be calm while things work themselves out.

Fine clothes may disguise, but foolish words will disclose a fool. (Aesop)

It's much more important to keep your mindfulness with you than your mobile phone. Mindfulness will do much more than a phone to protect you. Mindfulness will improve your communication.

Turn off the radio, the phone, the television. Turn off the thoughts in your head. Take refuge in the inner calm and peace of the quiet mind. Do not write, read, or surf the Internet. Keep still.

Remain open-minded with a sense of humor around closed-minded people; they think they are right.

Try taking the weekend off from computer screens. The world does not collapse when you don't check your e-mail for one or two days.

Let your friend talk. Avoid interrupting.
Don't take the stage from her. Don't try to
teach her anything. Be silent, or if she
wants feedback, paraphrase what she told
you without making a judgment.

In an argument, acknowledge the state of
mind by naming it and giving it space.
Shine the light of awareness on it and it
loses its power over you.

View information through insight. Try to
develop both intellect and intuition. Read
widely, think deeply, and retain your sense
of discrimination.

Even though we have two ears we can listen
to only one thing at a time.

Right Speech is also the healing practice of
silence.

Aim to be constructive, positive, empathetic. Give support and encouragement. Be open and sensitive to what others are experiencing and you will truly see and hear them.

Start a contemplative practice that combines meditation with self-reflection. This gives you a way of processing and gaining insight into the unspoken conversations within your own mind.

Are your explanations concise and to the point?

It's hard enough to speak mindfully under normal circumstances, but it is truly remarkable when you are able to hold steady during a painful moment.

Instead of constantly filling every gap in your conversations with meaningless chatter, learn how to pause and allow yourself to breathe, to reconnect with yourself.

Anger damages you. It makes you look ridiculous and feel miserable. When you let go of anger, love arises.

What would it take to simply forgive?

We're communicating in every moment, either with ourselves or with others. Thinking, speech, and bodily acts are our own manifestations.

Balance out a negative comment with a positive one.

Your job is to listen attentively, to put
    yourself in the other person's movie
    without interrupting and judging, no
    matter what he says.

Better than a thousand hollow words is one
    word that brings peace. (Buddha)

Notice the silence between sounds and the
    space between thoughts.

If you can write a letter that's full of
    understanding and compassion, then
    during the time of writing that letter you
    will nourish yourself.

He divides conversation into two categories:
    when you speak, and when you listen to
    yourself speak. (John Fowles)

You do not require perfect quiet to meditate. It isn't noise that bothers you; it is your judgment about the noise. Noise is no obstacle to meditation. Accept it. We live in a world of noise.

Your "mistakes" are a vital part of your learning. You discover how unskillful speech degrades personal relationships and diminishes the possibility of peace in the world.

Words can be gifts, words can be weapons, words can be magic, words can be prayer, poetry, or song.

Mindful communication means not only being as clear as possible, but as compassionate as possible. The tenet is nonharming—not engaging in any act that causes harm to yourself or others.

Try to not prepare and rehearse what you will say in advance, especially while someone else is speaking. Be in the present moment and speak what feels true and meaningful.

Pausing gives you a quick exit from the momentum of conversation and reconnects you with the present moment.

Use the ring of a cell phone or a red traffic light as a reminder to pause for a moment, take a deep breath, let your thoughts and words fall aside, and just listen.

Employing the precept of Right Speech also involves asking, What do I really value? What do I want? What is it that I love?

When one abstains from wrong speech, one speaks the truth, and uses words that are friendly, benevolent, pleasant, gentle, meaningful, and useful.

Opinion has caused more trouble on this little earth than all the plagues and earthquakes. (Voltaire)

In a difficult situation, open-ended questions encourage the speaker to express her feelings and may point the way to a solution.

Capable of practicing silence, you are free as a bird, in touch with the essence of things. Sometimes you have to practice silence. Silence is a time for looking deeply.

Reflective time provides a chance to focus inward and listen to the wise voice within.

Right Speech asks you to be aware of how you actually use the energy of your words.

After even a few weeks of meditation practice, you will find that your tendency to overreact in the face of your barriers is lessened.

According to one study, a typical information worker who sits at a computer all day turns to her e-mail program more than fifty times and uses instant messaging seventy-seven times per day.

Sit and listen to the quiet noises you can hear, the music of silence.

Listen for the sake of listening.

The temptation to vivify the tale and make it walk abroad on its own legs is hard to deny. (Gelett Burgess)

Analyzing even one reactive pattern helps you understand how you cut yourself off from friendliness when you shut down.

Whoever gossips to you will gossip about you. (Spanish proverb)

You have to protect yourself with the energy of compassion so that when you listen, instead of consuming toxins, you're actively producing more compassion in yourself.

All your actions and comments come back to you.

Listen with a still and concentrated mind.

Any one of us can create a culture of kindness in our lives by listening deeply to our own communication patterns and learning to be more encouraging.

It can be no dishonor / To learn from others when they speak good sense. (Sophocles)

Stop believing your inner critic.

Just as a mother would protect with her life her own child, so should one cultivate a boundless mind toward all beings and friendliness toward the entire world.

Wherever you are, listen. Bathe in the sounds around you and find a point of silence within.

The more you are driven to focus on helping others overcome suffering, the less you focus on your own suffering and the happier you become.

You would have peace if you would not concern yourself with the sayings and doings of others.

In a difficult situation, become aware of your breathing and the feelings or thoughts passing through you. Just by doing that, you may already calm down and the urge to speak mindlessly may pass.

Express only those thoughts that will bring
   happiness to yourself and others.

Can you recall the exuberance you felt the
   last time you had a captive audience? This
   is a gift you can give to others.

When you practice mindful communication,
   you become acutely aware of the sensitivity
   of your heart. Love opens you up, while
   fear shuts you down.

Whenever loved ones are angry and upset,
   your goal as listener is to help them feel
   understood, not put down.

Mindfulness shows you that everything you
   say is colored by your unique perceptions,
   your interpretations, and your emotional
   reactions.

Listening to establish a relationship with anyone requires that your concentration be flexible enough to shift into receiver mode and stay there, instead of being distracted by your own agenda.

When you are about to send an important e-mail or letter, stop for a moment. Pause. Then hit "Send" or put the letter in the slot with a feeling of confidence and trust.

Try listening to the way you sound to others. Are you using speech to manipulate emotions and feelings, yours or another's?

It's a simple equation. Wrong speech causes ill-being. Right Speech brings about well-being and healing.

It is always easier to blame someone else for your problems and hurt feelings than to acknowledge that there may be a fundamental wrongness in your own view.

Watch what you say over the fence.

Unwise speech causes heartbreak and separation; it makes enemies and creates fear.

Inwardly thank someone who disturbs or harms you with words or actions. Those who harm you are like teachers showing you the effects of your words and actions.

For a child, be present—even in silence— ready to listen without judgment and with an open mind.

Do not lie.

If every time you met with someone you gave her your full and complete attention for four minutes, come hell or high water, it could change your life.

You need Right Speech for the people you live with, the people you meet on the street, and other people you interact or work with.

First learn the meaning of what you say, and then speak. (Epictetus)

Being mindful of your speech is a key to becoming aware of your inner life and the quality of your relationships.

The greatest compliment that was ever paid me was when one asked me what I thought, and attended to my answer. (Henry David Thoreau)

Judge a person by both the good and bad they say, not just one.

When you listen to someone, give up all your subjective opinions.

Listen to a sound and come back to the present moment. Make the sound a bell of mindfulness calling you back to your center and the present moment.

Remember that people usually engage in negativity and excessive criticism out of feelings of jealousy, anger, or low self-esteem.

Spend at least five minutes of each meal in silence. If you do have a conversation, keep the topics light and supportive.

Speak when you are angry and you will make the best speech you will ever regret. (Ambrose Bierce)

The wisdom of karma, of cause and effect, teaches us that everything matters—every syllable, every sentence.

When we speak and act in a way that causes tension and anger, we are nourishing violence and suffering.

Forgive spoken words about you so your words are forgiven by others.

In listening, can you hear what is between the lines? Can you sense where the words are coming from? Can you perceive and even feel what others are feeling as they speak?

Ugly speech teaches ugly speech.

Eventually, mindfulness training can stabilize your mind so that you gain the power to align your speech with your intentions.

Think kindly, speak gently and clearly.

We do not talk—we bludgeon one another with facts and theories gleaned from cursory readings of newspapers, magazines, and digests. (Henry Miller)

When you are using the telephone, make sure your words create mutual understanding and love.

How bad can an insult be? Will any name you are called cause you lasting harm? Can't you just laugh it off, especially since most insults are exaggerations?

The heart of a fool is in his mouth, but the mouth of a wise man is in his heart. (Benjamin Franklin)

When you feel angry, do not say or do anything—just practice mindfulness.

Make yourself the designated listener.

If you know anything that is helpful and true, find the right time to say it. Do not speak impetuously. Think about it first; make sure that it will be helpful, that it's true, and that it's the right time.

You'll know the right time has come to say something when the other person is in a peaceful frame of mind and agreeable to listening.

People do not seem to talk for the sake of expressing their opinions, but to maintain an opinion for the sake of talking. (William Hazlitt)

If you have a wonderful idea and are eager to share it, that's good, but don't drown out others. Invite everybody to express their ideas and they will listen to yours.

Use speech to be a powerful motivator for good.

Regularly stop and ask yourself if you are moving in the direction of more honesty or not.

Accept that the other person's point of view that she has communicated has value.

Wise speech is both an ethical and a spiritual exploration. Committing yourself to wise speech, you learn to listen inwardly to the words beneath the words.

What we communicate is far deeper and more complex than just the concepts conveyed.

Your speech defines you.

Sometimes we tell ourselves stories or tell ourselves that something does not really matter even when we know it does.

Speech is based on thoughts. If you learn to be mindful of your thoughts, you will be mindful of your speech.

If you are about to complain about the temperature, stop. When cold, be thoroughly cold. When hot, be thoroughly hot. Be one with the environment. Accept it.

When someone asks you what you want, tell her.

It is a temptation to show how clever or funny you are by poking fun at someone or something, but it can be hurtful even in the guise of a joke.

For a day, vow to speak only what is truthful, helpful, and sensitive. Attune yourself to the words you speak and to how you listen.

In modern times, the positive and negative potentials of speech are vastly multiplied by the tremendous increase in the means, speed, and range of communications.

The Buddha said that speech that is dishonest, that puts others down, that is aimed at hurting other people's feelings or creating divisions, or that is essentially meaningless—causes us suffering.

What makes us use wrong and unskillful speech to others? Maybe we do it for entertainment, justification, or self-importance, or out of anger, or to seek bonding.

Hear the words, but let yourself savor the motivation behind the words.

We each have left a message or sent an e-mail that caused a problem. Often this could have been avoided if you had taken a minute to settle your mind before expressing yourself.

Value silence and its eloquence.

It is best to use language only when it is useful to do so.

See what happens if you simply watch and listen.

You can decide that anger and hatred serve no useful purpose and they are categorically destructive.

The energy you invest in restraining your anger needs to be more powerful than your concern for immediate goals or desires.

Whenever you have completed saying something, ask yourself whether what you have said resulted in well-being or harm. If it was harm, resolve never to make this mistake again.

Right Speech is abstaining from, or the intention to refrain from, lying, divisive speech, abusive or crude speech, and frivolous speech or chatter.

By listening mindfully and encouraging others, you can build a culture of kindness in your family, workplace, and community.

Your communication is not neutral. Every time you communicate, you either produce more compassion, love, and harmony or you produce more suffering and violence.

Wise speech is founded on your capacity to listen wholeheartedly.

At least once a day, tell your partner how terrific he or she is and that you love him or her.

When you do not say the positive things that need to be said, when you unconsciously say hurtful or meaningless things, and when you fail to address problems in your relationships directly and lovingly, suffering arises.

Nothing has the power to get us into more trouble than unwise speech. Wise speech is a practice in itself.

Better to remain silent and be thought a fool than to speak out and remove all doubt. (Abraham Lincoln)

Spend at least some time each day, even if it's only five or ten minutes, sitting, practicing mindful breathing, and listening to yourself.

To understand wise speech is a gift. It calls for immense mindfulness to know when to speak, when to be silent, how to speak words that touch the heart of another, and how to listen.

Silence protects your mindfulness practice, making it easier to pay attention to whatever you are doing in the present moment.

The link between elevating yourself and blaming others is sometimes hard to see. Both cause you to see yourself as separate from others.

Although you may feel irritation, do not lose yourself to anger. Be patient and don't react. Let go, accept, and forgive.

When you are listening to another but planning your own agenda at the same time, you are really talking to yourself and therefore not truly listening.

Be a person who says positive things about others.

If you practice sitting meditation, you start to appreciate that you can provide contentment and peace. Instead of the impulse to grasp something, you develop the discipline to simply let be.

The right word may be effective, but no word was ever as effective as a rightly timed pause. (Mark Twain)

Contemplate this classic Zen koan: Without speaking, without silence, how can you express truth?

Write to peel away layers of reactivity and access the depths of your soul. Unmask yourself and give shape to your experience.

What about the times when someone has made a mistake, but you exaggerate as though it's something many times worse?

Once your communication barrier is up, your mind stories start spinning. These justifications are how you give yourself permission to say or do something harmful.

Wouldn't it be wonderful if schools taught kids to calm and focus their minds a little, and then practice sitting down opposite another person and really paying attention to that person for a few moments?

One of the main reasons we listen poorly is because our internal noise levels are so turbulent and obtrusive that they mask most of what others are saying.

The Buddha taught that if you get in the habit of communicating in a meaningful and loving way, then you gradually develop certain inner qualities that give your words power and benefit others.

Wise speech is rooted in compassion and integrity. It protects the people you speak to as well as your own heart from guilt and remorse.

Entry-level Right Speech is speech that does not add pain to any situation. This means not telling lies or purposely using speech hurtfully.

Everyday life, whether at home, at work, or in the community, offers endless opportunities for bringing mindfulness and compassion to the arena of verbal interaction with others.

Take one aspect of Right Speech and practice it for a week: abstain from lying, abstain from speaking without care, abstain from gossiping in a way that creates negative energy.

The Dalai Lama says the main goal is to be kind. Stop before each action or word and weigh its kindness. Pay attention and give loving-kindness to your speech and actions.

Demonstrate an open mind by letting your opinions be positively interrupted by a moment of doubt.

Silent meditation helps train you to gently
let go of thoughts when they distract you.

Repetitive thoughts are messengers asking
for your attention. Ask yourself, Where
does simplicity lie in this moment? Listen
to the responses that arise within you.

Find that sweet spot between suppression of
and reaction with anger.

Let your words be in harmony with your
thoughts and intentions.

Soften by turning your attention to the
original pain that you've been avoiding.

I have often regretted my speech, never my
silence. (Publilius Syrus)

With inquisitive thinking, look closely and analyze what happens when a reaction starts to build; in that way you can recognize your blind spots.

A general instruction for silent practice is: No input, no output.

There is no point in trying to tell people things they cannot hear. Have patience.

When you don't want to appear weak and vulnerable, you say things that make you look strong and powerful.

Wise speech has the power to heal division, to foster love and trust, and to lead to intimacy.

Feeling angry is not wrong, but expressing anger in unproductive or hurtful ways is.

Be aware of anger, but do not see it as who you are.

Ask yourself, What is the best way to respond to the situation at hand? This causes a shift to happen and, though anger is present, you cultivate patience and acceptance.

Mindful listening helps you better understand the how and why of others' views. When understanding occurs, a sense of calm is achieved on both sides.

Calmness, an open mind, and focused attention are the foundation for mindful listening.

Meditation in action means being as highly aware of your words and intentions as you can. Make a total commitment to meditation in action in your communication with loved ones.

Your every utterance is heard more closely, interpreted more quickly, and acted on more directly than any other actions you take in your life. Your words should clearly and unequivocally express what you mean.

You don't always have to create artificial stimulation. Listen to the sound of silence.

Listening with a nonjudgmental and open heart is a way to bring loving-kindness into your communications.

Say no consciously and politely.

Even though what you have to say is important, you can respect what others find more important at the time.

Happiness comes when your work and words benefit both yourself and others. Karma says if you plant peaches, you will get peaches.

If there is one thing that any one of us could do that would automatically improve the quality of our relationships, it would be to become more conscious of what we say and how we say it.

Talking too much is quite often the result of the fear of silence.

Consider each word carefully before you say anything so that your speech is right in both form and content.

Write positive inspirational thoughts in a commonplace book.

Someone who can't understand and transform his own suffering makes the people around him suffer, too, even when that's not his intention. Because he suffers, you suffer. But he doesn't need punishment; he needs help.

If you can't control your mouth, there's no way you can hope to control your mind.

Select a period of time and resolve to become aware of your intentions to speak. What is the state of mind that immediately precedes talking?

Verbalize the positive.

Skillful speech entails speaking in ways that are comforting, peaceful, trustworthy, and worth hearing.

Skillful speech is a gift to others. People will listen more to what you say and they will be more likely to respond skillfully themselves.

Choose your words so they are always pleasant.

The ability to observe without evaluating is the highest form of intelligence. (J. Krishnamurti)

Decide that indulging in angry outbursts or negative speech would be a fate worse than death.

If truth can be cruel and foolish, lies and gossip are worse. They are worse than foolish honesty.

When e-mailing, just e-mail. When talking on your cell, just talk on your cell. (Soren Gordhamer)

A climate of scorn, blame, harshness, or rage is not an environment in which you find the trust or safety to listen, open your heart, or receive another.

Many disagreements can be resolved by acknowledging your barriers, trying to understand the disgruntled other, and connecting with your breath.

The flow of conversation hits a snag and you start editing information by either overreacting or underreacting to an event in the present moment. Recognize this.

Attentive to the feelings, intentions, and thoughts beneath your words, learn to cultivate the compassion, integrity, and kindness that bring harmony to your relationships and to your mind.

Do not say about others what you would not like said about you.

Share the best of yourself through your words. Try to avoid sharing the worst of yourself—blaming, criticizing, judgmental words. Use your words to support, not tear down.

Allow yourself to be positively interrupted by the basic wakefulness of your body so that you come back to your senses.

Even when spoken out of habit, abusive language fuels anger in ourselves and others.

Sit and listen quietly to all the sounds of your house that you are not usually aware of.

Speak gently and sincerely.

Try not commenting on anything said by the other person. Just listen. See how often your mind is busy preparing a response. Knowing that you are not going to respond can dramatically change the way you listen.

Speech can break lives, create enemies, and start wars. Speech can give wisdom, heal divisions, and create peace.

Words of love, tenderness, and kindness are urgently needed in a world saturated by so many unwise words.

When someone says something harsh or even unflattering, use your awareness to notice the words and count to ten before reacting and responding.

If you could listen to yourself as you converse, you would probably be surprised at how often you speak mindlessly.

Be aware of what you are saying and use loving speech. Listen deeply to the other person to hear what is being said and what is not being said.

Make scales and weights for your words, and put a door with bolts across your mouth. (Apocrypha, Ecclesiasticus)

Being civil and courteous with each other maintains a healthy boundary of aloneness, which is the antidote to mindlessness.

Begin by applying the golden rule of listening: Listen to others as you would have others listen to you.

One of the lessons to be learned from practicing mindful communication is the humble discovery of how easily any one of us can slip into these patterns of putting others down.

Do you remain silent when you could speak out?

After you have deeply listened and allowed the other person to express everything in his heart, you will have a chance later on to offer your own information—but not now.

Keep a journal of the kinds of thoughts that predominate. Notice the qualities associated with your thoughts. This will help you cultivate skillful thoughts.

One goal of compassionate communication is to help others suffer less.

Strive to avoid doing harm directly with your words (or deeds) or indirectly with your thoughts and intentions. Thoughts affect you internally and influence your way of interacting with others.

Without thinking and talking, there is no obstacle to get in the way of your enjoyment of the present moment.

Look at people when they speak to you.

Give yourself some silent time each day, for in moments of emptiness the spirit enters. Float in the emptiness of the silence. Let it fill your body and mind.

Unhitch the burden of belief systems (barriers) that prevent you from appreciating your differences from others.

Self-esteem grows from the respect that comes from being heard.

The mindful listener is free from the obsessive self-consciousness that interferes with the ability to concentrate. You feel happier and more positive when you are not focusing on the self.

Since you can never really take your words back, it is critical that you develop such mindfulness about your speech that you do not gossip in the first place.

The more you open to others and show love and compassion, the less you are obsessed with yourself and the more confident you become.

Relay an overheard compliment; forget an overheard criticism.

The more you listen, the more you will hear. The more you hear, the more deeply you will understand.

Never speak loudly to each other, unless the house is on fire.

Words of cruelty, harshness, dismissiveness, and anger linger long in the heart of the person they are spoken to. We carry deep wounds in our hearts that have been inflicted by words of anger.

Before sleep, review your day. Did you do, think, or say anything for which you feel regret? If so, think about whether anything needs to be put right. Do you need to make amends?

When you criticize others, the faults you find in them may be a reflection of your own fear. You may fear rejection, unworthiness, or lack of skill or intelligence.

When you cannot do anything external to change a bad situation, then you must work internally to change your perception of the situation so you do not react.

You might spend your whole day connecting
but not reduce the loneliness you feel.
When we feel empty, we sometimes use
technology to try to dissipate the feeling of
loneliness, but it doesn't work.

Speech should be wise, kind, and minimal.

Paraphrasing is the act of repeating back
your speaker's message for the purpose of
clarity and reflection.

When you are happily present in the present
moment, you are present for your spouse,
children, relatives, and friends.

Write a letter to your son or daughter.

One well-chosen word which brings the
listener peace is better than a thousand
spoken in vain.

Revive the lost art of conversation—
interesting, animated conversation.

Trying to speak with truth and honesty
helps make your speech simpler and wiser.

Meditation can help your mind become
calm and constant. Your mind can be
quiet and stable even though you are in
the midst of a noisy world.

Having a little quiet time when you can
relax and accept yourself as you are helps
you be more open to others.

The vast majority of problems in
relationships come from communications
that lack honesty, empathy, or love.

We are subject to many wrong perceptions
in our daily lives. Mindful communication
has the potential to ease much of the
unnecessary suffering in our relationships.

When you write words full of compassion and forgiveness, you feel freer, even if the person you're writing to hasn't read them yet.

Any reaction of frustration or fury does not change circumstances beyond your control. These reactions merely add internal suffering and stress to the pain and pressure you already feel.

The challenge is to keep from being changed by anger or propelled by it. If you cultivate tolerance and compassion, when anger arises it will not compel you to act unskillfully.

Improving communications within an organization is about developing better relationship skills through skillful speech and open listening.

Communications of any kind can be improved when the people involved become better listeners, speak from the heart, and observe how they interact with each other.

To stabilize attention, use a neutral object of some kind to gently bring awareness back whenever you drift off into thoughts. This could be an object in front of you or your own breath.

A great way to stimulate your creativity and spirituality is journal writing.

Pay attention to the words you speak and to their tone. Your words should reflect compassion and concern for others and should help and heal.

If you repeat the same story or opinion over and over again, it's probably because you don't feel heard. The repetition goes on in your mind and in your conversations. You want a listening partner who would simply be present for you.

Staying open even in conflict allows communication to flow both ways.

When you're listening to a coworker, be a witness to her ideas. Notice how you want to start judging. When this happens, put your mind in neutral and simply observe.

When you learn to listen mindfully, you can keep quiet long enough to respond rather than react.

Create a welcoming environment so that you can deeply listen to yourself.

If a speech act is motivated by true kindness, it will bring a positive result. Because karmic results do not always bear fruit immediately, it is sometimes difficult to observe this process in action.

The world can never be perfectly managed, but you can make peace with your lack of peace, learn to live with it, feel it, swim in it.

If you experiment with not talking about others who are not present, you will learn that a lot of your speech is judgment. By stopping this speech, your mind becomes less judgmental.

When we say something that nourishes us and uplifts the people around us, we are feeding love and compassion.

On the telephone, make certain that your words create mutual understanding and love. Have those words be as beautiful as flowers and gemstones.

Mastering yourself is true power.

Unsolicited advice sends the message that the receiver is not capable of solving his own problems; it is the ultimate put-down.

Ask yourself, Is my speech pure, flawless, and unblemished?

Acting while angry can lead to a lot of suffering and can escalate a problematic situation.

Stop frantically trying to have an opinion about what is going on and simply say, "Don't know." Live with this and the clouds of confusion will dissipate and your intuitions will become obvious.

It helps to use active listening skills such as mirroring back what you have heard or paraphrasing the ideas into your own words.

Each day, pause to do layered listening— hear the loudest, obvious sounds and then the next layer down, and so on.

To some extent, you habitually use words to express ego and a false self. You tell yourself and others stories about yourself and your life.

Asking for help when you are angry is very difficult, but it allows others to see your suffering instead of just your anger. Communication and healing can begin.

The realization of peace rests upon each of us learning to speak with wisdom.

When a person is given a chance to state his views without the threat of judgment or advice, even if his listener does not agree, that is the first step toward creating good feelings. This allows for discussion and problem solving.

Silence can be positive and comfortable, as when you are on a quiet beach looking out to sea and you feel the unseen energies of the place completely permeate your whole being.

After looking at the motivations behind your speech, notice the effect of the speech itself. What response do you get?

Once the mind is programmed to scan for hidden messages, it can do so automatically.

Silence is the threshold to the inner sanctum. Silence is the song of the heart.

A listener can positively interrupt to bring the speaker back to the present moment. A listener can also positively interrupt by simply mirroring back what she hears.

Rather than speaking badly about people and in ways that will produce only friction and unrest in their lives, you should speak of others' good qualities.

Distress from verbal communication could be markedly alleviated, even with difficult people, if we were more mindful of our words.

The wise ones fashioned speech with their thought, sifting it as grain is sifted through a sieve. (Buddha)

We don't want to be interrupted by silence or openness, because we feel we need mindless entertainment as a way of avoiding boredom.

Breathe deeply before you speak.

Take delight in the richness of language.

Once you understand that anger is your biggest enemy, it simplifies the struggle to discover happiness.

There is a way between voice and presence / where information flows. / In disciplined silence it opens. / With wandering talk it closes. (Rumi)

Why not take a day or a half-day to experience Noble Silence? Spend the time in your house, room, garden, or elsewhere without using any communication devices.

Make telephone calls with awareness and mindfulness.

Openness is how you stay connected with yourself just as much as how you connect with others. The way to cultivate this openness is by practicing mindful communication.

Cultivate kindness and gentleness in your speech.

What appears to you to be true may just be an opinion in disguise.

The only real control you have is choice of your own thoughts, your own words, and your own actions.

When intense reactions are taking hold of you, taking a break from the situation gives you a chance to return to the present moment.

In a contentious situation, you can redirect your mind to defuse your discomfort and frustration, using the energy to create mental "immunity" to the harmful situation.

Only love dispels hate. Only light can dispel darkness. Become silent, conscious, alert, aware, awake.

When angry, talk to yourself the same way you would talk to an upset friend.

Start the day by reaffirming your intention to speak with compassion and love.

Speak calmly instead of yelling.

It is always better to say something kind or encouraging than to speak sharply or derisively.

If you listen carefully, you will be able to really hear everyone.

You can vary what you say depending on how fragile you think someone might be about a certain subject. You want to tell the truth in a skillful way.

Each of us has experienced what happens when we have said something that was not true or genuine or beneficial. Being open, truthful, genuine, timely, and compassionate creates a sense of communion.

If you find yourself criticizing, analyzing, or interpreting what someone is saying, meet these thoughts with mindfulness. Let them go and return to listening.

Look to your tongue, for the greatest evils in human life come from it. (Cervantes)

He never labored so hard to learn a language as he did to hold his tongue and it affected him for life. The habit of reticence—of talking without meaning—is never effaced. (Henry Adams)

When you listen for the whole message, your senses need to be poised and focused, like a deer that freezes its gaze in the direction of a lurking predator.

Attune yourself to subtle changes in a speaker's tone, volume, and inflection.

Talk about what is bothering you instead of getting angry when others cannot read your mind.

Listen carefully to the voice in your mind as it is getting ready to make a comment and think to yourself, Why am I saying this?

Have you noticed how easy it is to be critical of people who are not present?

Before picking up the ringing phone, pause for a moment and let it ring one more time. Let the full ring complete itself. Listen to it. Compose yourself.

Are there times when your words may be true, but it is not the right time, place, or situation for them to be useful?

The statement "I understand that you believe this is true" shifts the focus away from the external situation and redirects attention to the belief system that is framing it.

Those who speak kind words are not always kind.

Distract yourself from a bad communication situation by counting your blessings, thinking about how things could be worse.

Omit needless words.

Start with wisdom, which tells you what is true and beneficial. Those things are worth saying.

If you wait until you have taken a few mindful breaths and returned to being fully present before you open an e-mail, your communication will be more effective, clearer, and more understanding.

Take a few deep breaths. Becoming aware of your breath helps you calm the mind because you are reflecting on the present moment.

When you are harmed on the verbal level, it can be a powerful cause of anger. You may take strong offense and become highly indignant.

You can create suffering through the stories you tell yourself. Your mind barrels along with a running commentary on everything, a constant judging of everything and everyone.

Right Speech requires being true to your word and not changing the content for your own advantage or to portray yourself in a better light.

Speak to your children with respect.

Speak your truth without trying to control others.

First practice mindful breathing and take care of your anger.

You have to use the tools of compassionate communication—deep listening and loving speech—to restore communication with the person with whom you are having difficulty.

I do know of these / That therefore only are reputed wise / For saying nothing. (Shakespeare)

When that clenching feeling happens, pause and stay open in the discomfort. If you can practice holding steady, accepting what you cannot change, you cut the root of the aggression.

Put a Post-it note next to the bed to remind yourself that tomorrow will be a day of Right Speech.

Let the outer chatter of the world pass you by.

She had lost the art of conversation but not, unfortunately, the power of speech. (George Bernard Shaw)

Not reading or writing for a day is a way to practice diminishing the incessant hum of thought and language. You can penetrate deeper into silence.

If someone you are communicating with suddenly shuts down, be flexible and abandon two-way communication. Shift into the one-way street of mindful presence.

Improving on silence is hard to do with speech.

Before you speak, ask yourself: Is this kind, is it necessary, is it true, and does it improve upon silence?

Practicing mindful communication is a way to make room on your path to learn something from every conversation that occurs in your life, pleasant or unpleasant.

The way to find more happiness is to take the causes that usually bring suffering and transform them into causes of happiness. How? Change your reaction. Tolerance is the start of freedom.

Before judging and shouting at somebody, instead of telling someone she has no value, you must be quiet and look deeper.

One of the benefits of meditation is that you learn to pause before you speak.

Talk late into the night when someone needs it.

Speaking good about someone behind her back gets back to her just as quickly as speaking badly.

Watch your words; they become your actions.

When you listen with compassion, you don't get caught in judgment. A judgment may form, but you don't hold on to it.

The next time you say something you regret, notice whether you were propelled by self-consciousness, ego fulfillment, or disrespect for the other person's perspective. Smile at your newfound awareness, knowing that this discovery will prevent future mindless moments.

Notice how much more appropriate your
comments are when you are mindful not
only of your intent, but also of the
perspective of your listener. You will say
less and learn more.

Pay attention to what drives you to speak
critically.

You should never knowingly speak a lie, for
your advantage, someone else's, or any
reason whatsoever. Telling lies arises from
an inability or unwillingness to see the
situation as it is.

Before you speak, ask yourself: Are you
about to be helpful or harmful? Are you
about to be skillful or unskillful? Are you
about to be selfless or selfish? Are your
words filled with loving-kindness?

Give accurate feedback.

When you listen mindfully to others, you help quiet down their internal noise.

If you can't accept yourself—if you hate yourself and get angry with yourself—how can you love another person and communicate love to her?

If you communicate a lot during your actual work time, try to limit your communication during your work breaks.

When someone starts to tell you about a problem that neither of you can do anything about, say, "Why don't you not tell me about this before we both become upset about it?"

When you are caught in judging mind, you criticize. Pointing out mistakes, you think you feel better about yourself. But this feeling is based on fear, the fear that you may make similar mistakes.

Punctuate your words with space.

Learn to speak the words that you wish to hear, words that you will not later regret. Learn to speak simply and wisely.

To improve communication, clarify what you hear by paraphrasing.

Unless there is loving-kindness in your speech, it is going to come out wrong.

His first theory was that if human beings didn't keep exercising their lips, their mouths probably shriveled up. After a few months of observation he had come up with a second theory, which was this—"If human beings don't keep exercising their lips, their brains start working." (Douglas Adams)

Let someone else have the last word.

You absorb the thoughts, speech, and actions you produce and those contained in the communications of those around you.

Mouth "I love you" across a room.

Learn from all, judge no one, be kind to all, and say thank you.

Talk gently, sweetly.

We spend so much of our lives talking, analyzing, discussing, gossiping, planning. Most of this talk is not very conscious or aware.

Remember that barriers to communication cut you off not only from others but also from yourself.

Mindfulness enables you to use every small disappointment as a training ground for the big ones around the corner.

Don't chatter and use words to fill empty spaces with noise.

Offering a calm and gentle smile is an act of peace. Speak peacefully, walk peacefully, think peacefully, and your peace will radiate out in all directions.

There is great skill involved in learning how to listen. Courtesy is most precious. Be open and accepting of others.

Right Speech is about paying attention to your speech, seeing how and when your words are connected to your heart.

Feeling isolated, you may drown yourself in the idle chatter of radio, stereo, or other background noise. This does not ease the loneliness but, rather, agitates your mind and heart.

Appreciate nonverbal communication.

At least once each day, try to listen to others without judgment.

Cultivating kindness, sensitivity, and gentleness in your speech is a direct result of cultivating patience, tolerance, and respect in your heart.

Cultivate a way of speaking that is simple and spare.

A pause changes your response. You might decide to have a calm conversation with someone who has annoyed you. You might choose to leave the room until you cool down. You might choose to focus on your breath to regain balance and perspective.

You should always tell the truth. Even if you think it is a small lie or one that will help someone, you should still tell the truth. Lying contradicts reality, so it will never help.

The agitated mind is the forerunner of agitated speech, and the mind of calmness and simplicity is the forerunner of speech that communicates openness and sensitivity.

It is not always easy to find the wisdom and humility to say "I don't know."

Have you known people whose ego was so overpowering that they could not stop speaking? Help such a person by treating him with loving-kindness and compassion.

Accusations and verbal abuse directed at another become a means of relieving yourself of the pain of your own anger. You insist on being heard, yet in doing so you create deeper pain.

Unkind words can never be taken back and they leave the residue of pain and fear in another's heart.

Karma is made of three elements: thought, speech, and actions.

Offer advice only when asked, and then with compassion.

Listen to a sound, from beginning to end.

When you intend to speak, first examine your mind and then act appropriately with composure.

Let your good words be discovered by accident.

Practice letting go of the desire to speak when it is not really necessary.

So much of what you say every day is driven by attachment, aversion, and ignorance.

The practice of Right Speech also concerns your inner dialogue, the endless speech going on inside your head.

True listening is a way of stopping and being present so that whatever is being said is immediately apparent. Try just being present without judgment or preconception.

Another way to intervene during a blaming conversation is to use reflective listening to mirror back the facts without coloring them with your personal evaluation.

Work to take responsibility for the anger and fear that arise in your heart, rather than disguising them as opinions and judgment.

If you speak ill of one person, you probably speak ill of many people.

Whenever your attention strays into thoughts, gently interrupt it by saying "Thinking" and return to your object.

Seek to use words that make a difference.

When you practice Right Speech, your words become a gift to others. People will start listening more to what you say, and will be more likely to respond in kind.

The way you act in the present moment shapes the world of your experience.

If you maintain mindfulness, nothing will upset you. You will not become angry or agitated. You can be patient no matter what anyone says or does. You can stay peaceful and happy.

Write for ten minutes about what you have learned from a negative experience.

Anger often makes us hurt ourselves more than any enemy.

Trained in patience, when a moment of anger arises in your everyday life, you might be able to hold your speech and action. You don't jump, lash, or act out.

If you are really dedicated to practicing patience, you even learn to generate love and compassion on the spot when anger arises.

Refrain from speaking about any third person not present. Undertake for one week not to gossip positively or negatively, or to speak about anyone you know who is not present with you.

When you don't feel you can communicate well in person or you wonder if what you say will be hard for the other person to hear, you might write a thoughtful letter or e-mail.

To enrich a challenging situation, you often need to absorb insults and emotional injuries while waiting for a flash of openness to occur in the other person.

Open yourself to your own distress signals and you will cut through the confusion of your thoughts like an "Aha" moment when you see something you didn't understand before.

A person's heart dictates what she says.

Make a statement, hear it back in your head, and study your listener to be sure it was received the way you meant it.

Speak from the reality of your life, not from concepts or ideas. Speak about the present reality. Stay in the present moment.

Ask yourself, Do I seek out meaningful, fulfilling relationships and connections or do I gravitate toward people who pull me away from my spiritual path?

The best thing about animals is that they don't talk much. (Thornton Wilder)

Exploring the path of wise speech is an invitation to find your own voice. It is a voice of authenticity rooted in your personal experience and wisdom.

Use the mantra "Filter" or "Pause" to take a moment to stop and ask yourself whether what you are about to say is beneficial to anyone.

Listen to the whole answer.

If it will brighten someone's day, say it.

Learn how to stop talking when there is nothing more to say.

Sometimes one cruel utterance can make the other person suffer for many years, and you will suffer for many years, too.

Even if it's just a short note, everything you write can nourish you and the person to whom you are writing.

When someone tells you about her goal, point out possibilities, not obstacles.

If you listen carefully, you can learn from the most subtle whispers of thought and sensation as well as the most overwhelming feelings and emotions.

Ask yourself: Who is making me angry? Am I mad at myself? No one can make us angry if we have no seeds of anger inside us.

If you practice consistently saying what is true in an honest and loving way, again and again, over time it can bring about deep changes for people you constantly interact with as well as for yourself.

Take your time and don't say things impulsively.

It requires a sense of calm to rationally deal with the onslaught of verbal conflict.

Often at work we don't give ourselves time or space to recognize and embrace strong emotions, so our tension comes out in unintentional ways. This can make communication difficult.

The three qualities of Right View, Right Mindfulness, and Right Effort run with and circle around Right Speech.

More often than not, what you say and how you say it determine the quality of your relationships.

The tongue, like a sharp knife, kills without drawing blood. (Buddha)

Save yourself from saying things you will later regret.

Let the other person know you are truly interested in what he is saying by asking questions instead of offering suggestions. Share your experiences only if they are relevant.

Simply notice the effects that all your conversations—both external and internal—have on you.

When reassurance is sincere, accompanied by a warm voice and a simple gesture, it is appreciated.

Reading makes a full man, meditation a profound man, discourse a clear man. (Benjamin Franklin)

Pass on some good news—but don't pass on gossip.

When you have a constant dialogue with yourself, become aware and say to yourself, "Stop talking."

In a conversation, keep in mind that you're more interested in what you have to say than anyone else is. (Andrew Rooney)

In learning to listen inwardly, you learn to pause before assuming that any of your conclusions or opinions are absolutely true.

Call your two favorite people to tell them how wonderful they are.

Kind words and actions are their own reward.

Instead of dwelling on self-assessment (usually filled with negative self-talk), you might be happier listening to someone else.

Note the intentions that motivate your speech. Look at your state of mind that precedes talking, the motivation for your comments and responses. Do this observation without any judgment.

Note the effect of your speech. What kind of response does it get—compassion or love? Irritation? If your speech is mindless, on automatic pilot, what is the response?

Ask yourself, Do I have the inner strength to respond intelligently and gently to the diversity of opinions that exists in the world?

It is possible to use speech to become awake. You can become mindful of what you are doing when you speak, the motivation, how you are feeling.

Let your speech follow a good and honest heart.

Tell a friend, "You did great!"

You may be hiding behind the stories you tell yourself and others to get what you think you want. This just makes you feel incomplete and alienated from your authentic self.

As your mind becomes more trained, you can use this skill in conversation by resting your attention on another person's body language and voice.

Be sure your mind is engaged before putting your mouth into gear. Be aware of what you are saying while you say it. This is mindful speech.

Remember to be gentle, patient, and encouraging with yourself and others in this lifelong practice of transforming conversations into a path of wakefulness.

A good listener avoids any selfish attempt to interrupt the speaker's stream of consciousness.

He who speaks without modesty will find it difficult to make his words good. (Confucius)

Mindful self-listening means answering questions directly, choosing topics that are appropriate to the conversation, and selecting your words carefully so that they reflect your true meaning.

Listening is an attitude of the heart, a genuine desire to be with another which both attracts and heals. (J. Isham)

Your words ideally will become a reflection of your desire to help others.

Think about the people you easily open up to. Then think about a person you find frustrating to speak with. You will discover in both cases that their manner of responding is a major factor.

Our speech is powerful. It can be destructive or enlightening, idle gossip or compassionate communication.

Each day, tell someone that you like or appreciate something about her.

Be careful of the words you use, and keep them short and sweet, as you never know from day to day which ones you will have to eat.

If the quality of your listening is not good enough, it's better to pause and continue another day.

Reflect on all of the times you open your mouth and speak for no reason at all—out of habit, to fill a silence. Noise surrounds us all the time, as if people are afraid of silence.

Never separate the life you live from the words you speak. (Paul Wellstone)

We distract ourselves from what is most real in order to lull ourselves and others into a sort of waking sleep.

If someone asks you a question and you do not know the answer, respond that you "don't know" and avoid making a problem of not knowing. See it as the truth of the moment.

A sage thing is timely silence, and better than any speech. (Plutarch)

You need to practice nourishing compassion in yourself so that you can be well equipped for listening.

Daily mindfulness practice makes it comfortable and natural to take in the whole message and choose your words carefully in much less time and with greater accuracy.

If you stop running and listen closely, you may hear the voice of your own inner wisdom.

Before you open your mouth, learn to pause and listen to yourself.

Talk to children at their eye level.

What keeps you from speaking the truth or speaking from the heart? Fear—especially fear of not being loved or admired. We also fear rocking the boat, upsetting people, and being exposed.

We think that if we speak the truth, we will get in trouble. We need to learn how to express ourselves, how to see things and let them go and not get caught up in them.

In your conversations, recognize when you are using justifications, refusing feedback, blaming, complaining, silencing, suppressing, and bullying. Pause. Once you pause, you refrain from causing harm.

Your words should be coherent and controlled, clear and pleasant, and spoken in a calm and gentle voice.

Abandon words and live your own Zen.

It is likely that your internal and external talk run in parallel tracks. Both can be heard and heeded. If you can hear and improve your internal monologue, it will benefit you and others.

Ask yourself if you need to express an opinion or make a comment.

Talk when necessary and use words that are sweet.

You will not lose yourself to anger if you can tolerate an irritation, be patient with the harm and the person harming, refrain from reacting vengefully, and then forgive.

Tell someone how great he looks.

If you bring your awareness to mindful breathing and to what's happening right in that moment, you can enjoy every moment of getting to your destination.

Speak words that create peace, are pleasant to hear, and are spoken at the proper time. Speak only what is true and useful.

Why is it important to put aside your agenda when listening to someone else? So that you can hear what the other party is saying.

Let your heart demonstrate tenderness by being positively interrupted by a flash of empathy.

If you approach a listening opportunity with the same self-abandonment as you do at the movies, think of how much more you stand to gain from such encounters.

By demonstrating compassion in your speech and treating others as you would like to be treated, you can ease difficult experiences they may be encountering.

Make a conscious effort to relax your breathing during conversations.

Respond to anxiety with action.

We oftener say things because we can say them well, than because they are sound and reasonable. (Walter Savage Landor)

Your words can inspire confidence and openness in another person. Generosity can be practiced with loving speech. You don't have to spend any money to practice generosity.

Do you take the time to listen before you speak?

If you want to make other people happy, choose your words carefully.

Speak slowly enough to stay mindfully connected with yourself.

Never explain—your friends do not need it and your enemies will not believe you anyway. (Elbert Hubbard)

Suffering does not befall him who is unattached to words.

If you act angry long enough, you become angry. And using harsh speech a lot is acting angry.

Practicing restraint with small desires gives you the strength to be restrained when there are more powerful, harmful desires.

It is proof of high culture to say the greatest matters in the simplest way. (Ralph Waldo Emerson)

Speak clearly, if you speak at all; / Carve every word before you let it fall. (Oliver Wendell Holmes, Sr.)

Do not harm someone's reputation.

It takes a genius to whine appealingly. (F. Scott Fitzgerald)

Next time you are about to lose it, be aware of the body sensations (heat, flush of anger, knot in stomach). Ask yourself if what you are about to say will be harmful. If your answer is yes, don't say it.

Each complaint lays the ground for the next complaint. What is the point of complaining or criticizing? A clearer, more direct request or suggestion may help alleviate a problem.

Using words to destroy your enemy, you destroy yourself as well.

Do you have the patience to wait until the mind settles and the water is clear? Can you be quiet for a moment, until the right words arise by themselves—honest words that do not hurt others?

What you say to yourself shapes the relationship you have with yourself. What you say to others shapes your relationships with the rest of the world.

The quiet of nonthinking and nontalking gives you the space to truly listen to yourself.

Even if someone slanders and criticizes you or spreads cruel rumors, speak of that person with kindness. Reply with kindness and compassion to negativity and harm.

Right Speech means abstention from telling lies, from backbiting and slander and talk that may bring about hatred, enmity, disunity, and disharmony among individuals or groups of people.

Right Speech is abstention from harsh, rude, impolite, malicious, and abusive language. It is abstention from idle, useless, and foolish babble and gossip.

With good internal communication facilitated by mindful breathing, you can begin to understand yourself, understand your suffering, and understand your happiness.

Being honest does not mean being hurtful. Being mindful does not always mean being nice. If you are honest and mindful, you will act from kindness of heart.

Among others, keep a check on your speech.
/ When alone, keep a check on your mind.
(Atisha)

Gentle speech tempers your reactions by
meeting your uncomfortable, irritating, or
painful experiences with compassion,
insight, and attention.

Try to keep the three doors—your body,
your mouth, and your mind—as pure as
possible in the practice of karma.

Never speak of yourself to others; make
them talk about themselves instead:
therein lies the whole art of pleasing.
Everyone knows it and everyone forgets it.
(Edmond and Jules de Goncourt)

Develop a silent prayer: Silence is true,
silence is grace, silence is golden, silence is
medicinal, silence heals, silence is real.
Silence is within you.

I'm glad I understand that while language is a gift, listening is a responsibility. (Nikki Giovanni)

Imagine how successful and effective you could be if you would let yourself experience that sense of total absorption in every listening opportunity.

The next time you have the urge to interrupt someone, pause. Instead, really listen to the complete thought(s) expressed. Don't just wait for the other person to finish talking so you can interject.

Be quick to listen, and deliberate in giving an answer. If you understand the matter, give your neighbor an answer; if not, put your hand over your mouth. Both honor and disgrace come from talking; a man's tongue can cause his downfall. (Apocrypha, Ecclesiasticus)

Silent practice helps you learn to stop your own noise. The practice of silence helps you learn to hear, helps you develop awareness.

Speaking gently increases the chances that what you say will be heard.

When a child speaks, really listen.

Whenever your mind tries to dwell on negative information, take time to silently clear your head.

Speak wisely, responsibly, and appropriately.

People are often uncomfortable trying to communicate feelings. By listening deeply, taking time to breathe, you can avoid conditioned reactions. You can respond compassionately.

Your communication is what you put out into the world and what remains after you have left it. In this way, your communication is your karma.

Why spend so much time trying to be right about so little?

Stop from time to time during the day and pay attention to your inner dialogue. You are not your thoughts and you need to get used to *not* believing the messages they give.

Listening is like pouring tea into a cup. When the cup is clean and empty, you are able to hear what the other person is saying clearly.

Yelling and punching your pillow can be just rehearsing and nourishing anger and making it stronger, not getting it out of your system.

During the day, there are opportunities to seek and touch the silence underneath.

Silence tunes you in to your natural communication system, the intuitive way of knowing that flows beyond the level of words.

No one means all he says, and yet very few say all they mean. (Henry Adams)

If the content of your speech is not authentic, talking or texting on a device doesn't mean you're truly communicating with another person.

The spaces between your words are often more profound than the chatter.

Stop an argument in your mind before opening your mouth.

Speech must be useful or beneficial.

When you are irritated by someone, see what qualities you find irritating. Notice if these qualities exist in you as well. Focus less on how that person should change and more on what lessons you can learn.

Communicate your needs, ideas, and opinions in a positive way.

Be aware of yourself as someone looking and listening. These are two of your most common activities, but normally you focus on what you perceive and not on the experience of listening.

Find ways to keep your words gentle, loving, accurate, and positive—even when you are annoyed or upset.

Try not to complain, especially about things that are not likely to change. Even complaints tempered with humor do not serve any purpose. Try to alleviate problems with action.

If you are not able to speak calmly, don't speak.

Purposely turn down the volume on the television. Put all your attention on what the person on television is saying. Challenge your ability to concentrate in noisy situations that are not under your control.

Silently endure.

The voices of judgment, ambition, perfection, fear, and abandonment shout within you, diminishing your capacity for listening.

Along with a goodnight kiss, tell your child you appreciate all the good things he or she did that day.

You can say, "I want to listen to you when I'm at my best. Would it be all right if we continued tomorrow?"

When you realize the danger of giving over to hatred and anger in reaction to some injury done to you, you experience the benefits. You end the violence and keep your happiness.

Speaking honestly needs to be linked to a heart of kindness and compassion.

Forgiveness comes from a deep longing to restore a sense of balance and wholeness to your relationships and your community.

A day of Right Speech can only help your karma.

If you listen in mindfulness with a nonjudgmental ear, you will naturally respond in a way that encourages open and satisfying communication.

When you suffer, you think it's the other person's fault for not appreciating you enough or loving you enough.

Speech does not inflict real pain, unless you let it.

Let your children overhear you complimenting them to other adults.

If you want to know why your kids don't talk to you, why people avoid striking up a conversation with you, start by identifying your most frequent response types.

Always leave loved ones with loving words.

Counter with the positive.

Express yourself at the right time, at the right place, with the right words and the right attitude.

Next time you talk to someone, relish the pauses and also the trust flowing within the conversation.

You should remain silent if doing so will prevent harm to another being.

A man must not always tell all, for that were folly: but what a man says should be what he thinks. (Montaigne)

You develop the power to genuinely encourage others by meeting your own self-doubts with kindness.

Unskillful communication is a leading cause of family tension and problems. When you are with your family, try giving yourself some mini-occasions to breathe mindfully and relax.

Listen with compassion, without judgment, and with an open mind.

When acting as an intermediary between arguing friends, promote harmony and unity. Refrain from allowing your attachments and expectations to cause or further an argument.

In a time of crisis, simply be present with whatever occurs, fully there, without judgment or prejudice. Again and again, use mindfulness to see whatever it is just as it is.

You can change your way of responding, not by memorizing a new list of tricks or acting differently, but by listening to yourself and becoming aware of the impact of your behavior.

When your mouth offers only wisely chosen speech, you sow beautiful seeds in the garden of your heart and life.

Learning to carefully select your words plays a major role in presenting yourself in a favorable light, getting along well with others, and effectively getting the job done.

The more you become familiar with your reactions to uncertainty, the less power they have to throw you off course.

The words you speak are pivotal to the kind of relationships you form and how you touch the hearts of others.

Treat your listeners with courtesy and respect.

As you practice Right Speech, try to be open, still, and aware of what others are thinking and feeling.

When one word has the power to make you hot and angry, why should not another word have the power to heal?

Work toward stopping the internal dialogue, the constant comment of the mind, breaking through where the thinking occurs and directly experiencing the process.

When you stop the internal dialogue, you create the ability to wait and to listen.

What is timely speech? It is speech not driven by impulsivity and it rests on a foundation that creates a good chance of its being truly heard.

Let go of wasteful speech and idle gossip.

Take a breath. Look inside where it is quiet. Meditate on it.

Being able to listen attentively is the most important skill in communication.

Return kind words for negative as often as possible.

We often talk about things that don't have much meaning to us or to the people we are talking with.

If you have any prior notice of an impending confrontation, prepare with a few deep, slow breaths and continue breathing slowly and fully as you listen.

A word and a stone let go cannot be called back. (Thomas Fuller)

After you ask for guidance—listen!

Watch what you say.

Only an unhappy person acts in a nasty and mean way. A happy person acts and speaks in a happy way and will not make others angry.

The person you are so angry with is suffering, experiencing unhappiness. Have some compassion for her suffering.

Patience means taking a few deep breaths instead of yelling in frustration.

Take advantage of a bad situation to develop your tolerance and strength. See through your original sense of certainty about what is wrong, and try viewing the situation from another perspective.

Realize that getting upset is not going to improve the bad situation; it will only add to your frustration and unhappiness.

Swear words or obscenities are a turnoff and suggest an inability to express yourself in a more intelligent manner.

Gather the courage to genuinely love other people as they are, rather than as you wish they could be.

Wise and simple speech is one of the hardest of all the branches of mindfulness.

Listen calmly.

Questions that attack, criticize, or make assumptions come across to the listener as punitive.

If your partner says something untrue, don't interrupt. Let him speak. Look deeply, in order to skillfully tell him about his wrong perception when he can hear it.

Examining your habitual responses to others helps you better understand your attitude toward listening to others.

Sit down and write continuously for ten or twenty minutes. Anything that comes into your head should be written down. Don't judge, analyze, or interpret. Let the words flow.

When you engage with someone you do not know, such as the grocery store cashier, be present with that person. A connection exists and you are simply opening your mind to see it.

You need to use your mind skillfully to unravel your entrapment in words and ideas. You can strip away what covers deeper reality.

One of the lessons of history is that nothing is often a good thing to do and always a clever thing to say. (Will Durant)

See the danger of conversations that lead nowhere. Trust what need not be said.

People often speak in order to distract themselves and others from what is most essential in that moment.

A person with integrity and confidence does not need to shout; her silence speaks as loud as her words.

Center and collect yourself each time you speak. Be mindful of all your words. Be conscious of your tone of voice and whether you are saying what you really want to say.

Use a bell, chime, or other reminder to deliberately interrupt your conversations and activities.

Ask someone who is agitated, "Is there anything else that has upset you?" This type of question will let the other person know you were listening closely.

Try putting this book down for a moment,
and simply feel present in your body.
Notice all your perceptions. This presence
is what interrupts thoughts and brings you
back to your senses.

Try to make at least one person feel better
each day because of something you say.

It is skillful to focus on and cultivate the
positive in life. Do not blot out the
negative, but spend more of your time and
energy on the positive.

Write a haiku. It is creating a word
photograph. No emotion, no judgment, no
interpretation. It is a snapshot of a
moment, capturing a moment of reality.

Spoken words are never without
consequences.

The goal is to be mindful and aware in all conversations and interactions.

If you don't want others to think poorly of you, then don't get angry at their insults or harsh words. Ignore attempts to provoke you; maintain a cheerful attitude in spite of others' hostility.

Say nice things to people.

If you are in a relationship where both people love each other and don't intentionally hurt each other, you still may have miscommunications. Focus on using compassionate speech and deep listening.

You will catch more flies with honey than with vinegar.

Reactions such as silencing or blaming are really forms of bullying others or ourselves. Bullying does not protect us.

If a heart and mind is filled with compassion and loving-kindness, there is no room for hate or anger.

If yesterday you said something that wasn't right, do something today to transform it.

With mindful breathing and listening, your capacity for listening and looking expands deeply, and you may find the opportunity for much greater communication and connection.

Complaint is frustrating and painful. Narrowing your mind with complaint is unpleasant and claustrophobic. Complaint is the by-product of an untamed mind.

Avoid telling stories and opening up topics that are of interest only to you.

In a good relationship, both people usually keep their mouths shut half of the time they want to speak.

The more productive method of communicating your interests would be to sit back and make an effort to listen.

Allow others to finish speaking before you say anything.

Using mindfulness, you can note, "This is anger." Then, if you decide to speak or act, you can do so from a place of acknowledging those feelings.

Right Speech is speech that is in some way compassionate or kind or useful to someone.

Speak only when your words are better than your silence.

It is important to have pure intentions and express yourself from the heart. Be patient and prepared to persevere.

Compassionate listening isn't the only thing you can do when someone is suffering, but it's almost always the first step.

Angry comments by someone are usually requests for more attention. When you are subjected to angry speech, you can usually end the situation by listening—really listening—instead of reacting.

Truly listening, forgetting yourself for a short time and getting into the speaker's movie, can be the kindest gift you can give to another.

With a practice of breathing mindfully, walking mindfully, and looking deeply you can bring about transformation and restore communication in even the most difficult families.

Thinking is the speech of your mind. Right thinking makes your speech clear and beneficial.

Your words are your thoughts with wings. You open your mouth and your mind flies out.

Before you speak, you think. Before you think, you feel. How you feel is linked to your past experience, memories, and preferences—and to your conditioning and state of mind in that moment.

Let a challenging situation go. Don't dwell on it or complain about it, especially when it will change and dissipate. You might create bad karma with your thoughts.

[S]tart each day by affirming peaceful, contented, and happy attitudes and your days will tend to be pleasant and successful... Watch your manner of speech then if you wish to develop a peaceful state of mind. (Norman Vincent Peale)

When you sit down and meditate, you learn how to trust yourself. You witness the ongoing conversations in your mind without buying into them.

You reach out to others through your speech, asking to be acknowledged, seen, heard, and connected.

Letting go means staying awake to the boundaries of reality—the truth that, as much as you want to, you can't capture these beautiful moments and freeze them forever.

Even if someone criticizes you, speak of that person with kindness. Reply with kindness and compassion to negativity and harm.

Ask yourself before you speak: Is it true? Is it kind? Is it beneficial? Does it harm anyone? Is this the right time to say anything?

Occupy yourself with living life, not just talking about it.

Never underestimate the power of love, the power of forgiveness, the power of a kind word or deed.

Recognize when the channel of communication has shut down. With that awareness you remain silent instead of blurting out something you will later regret.

If friends, family, and coworkers avoid connecting with you, it may be that you have allowed self-interest, prejudice, negativism, and status to take control of your conversations.

Refuse to listen to others gripe and complain.

Talk to people as if they are doors, not walls. If they are doors, they will listen and they will be ready to absorb what you say. If you look at them as walls, then there will be no way to communicate with them effectively.

If you can restrain yourself from responses that impose self-judgment—advice giving, interrogation, and denial—your tendency to prejudge and discriminate may lessen.

In a conflict, when your opponent is engaged in the see-saw pattern of divisiveness, invite your opponent into a cooperative stance.

Is what you want to say either helpful or needed?

A bully is someone who is so unhappy with himself that he takes his own sadness and anger out on others. Bullies always use wrong speech.

Speak according to the mind of the person who listens and the ability of that person to receive what you share.

When we are angry and speak harshly to others, we lose our spiritual footing. We create pain, causing someone else's mind to become disturbed and upset.

The first step in dealing with someone else's aggression is to hold steady with your own serenity. Describe the problem accurately to yourself, without exaggerating.

The peace you discover in an unclouded mind and heart is manifested in your speech and also in the growing peace and confidence in your relationships with others.

Communicate in a way that fosters connection rather than divisiveness.

Mindful listening includes the ability to listen to what you say and make necessary changes.

Blessed is the man who, having nothing to say, abstains from giving us worthy evidence of the fact. (George Eliot)

After you have been able to say something kind, forgiving, and compassionate, you feel much better.

Sometimes we are more interested in setting a person straight than in taking care of our own anger. We are like the person chasing the arsonist instead of going home to put out the fire.

Respond to loneliness by connecting.

When someone irritates you, you might want to attack. You have to disentangle yourself from the unhappiness and go back to your peace until you know how to handle the situation in a loving way.

Make a phone call to tell someone the good thoughts you've had about her.

Intentionally bring gaps into your conversations, opening the space for genuine listening.

Noticing yourself shift from open to fearful and then to closed communication enables you to recognize this process in someone else.

You may not be able to avoid difficult situations, but you can lessen your suffering by how you choose to respond to the situation.

Talking disparagingly about a third person is ugly. Talking admiringly about a third person might cause the listener to feel unimportant. Do neither.

No matter how messed up you feel, you have goodness at your core. Once you have seen how much better it is to do good than to do evil, you will trust in your own inherent goodness.

A courageous first step for dissolving barriers is to be willing to look more closely at your patterns, the chain reactions that turn your original pain into a secondary layer of aggression.

Those who choose not to be so rigid about people and things, seeing all approaches as necessary for the balance of the common good, turn out to be the best listeners.

Be the first to say hello or give a kiss.

Anger and excessive fear throw you off balance and exhaust you, making you more vulnerable to an enemy attack.

Give yourself time before the day begins to let go and do some creative writing.

Be aware of what you are saying while you say it.

We express our anxiety and discomfort in social situations through mindless speech. We ramble and prattle on without any real awareness. We are filling the void of our fear and anxiety with words.

If you are a chronic interrupter, halt your interruption midsentence and say, "Excuse me. Please go on with what you were saying." In time, you will catch yourself before you interrupt.

A great way to demonstrate love to another person is to be completely present for that person.

Next time you hold the phone, look at it and remember that its purpose is to help you communicate with compassion.

Not knowing how to touch the heart of another and forge loving, meaningful connections, you may speak words that leave you isolated or frustrated.

Use the power of words to build deeper connections. The connections you make with others, superficial or profound, most often begin with the spoken or written word.

During the day, whenever something ruffles or disturbs you, recall an image of a mountain lake. Feel its ripples, and then let them settle.

You can begin the practice of restoring communication by modeling openhearted, compassionate dialogue.

Shut up, shut up, shut up, shut up, shut up, shut up. To talk a lot unnecessarily is like allowing thousands of weeds to grow in a garden. It would be better to have a flower.

Tolerating discomfort gives you the ability to endure, which leads to an inner release from the force of circumstances, making real happiness possible.

You can turn every phone conversation or e-mail into an opportunity to practice compassionate communication.

We speak a lot in life. We talk so much to each other. Right Speech can make things clear, help us to see, to let go, to discover, to awaken.

It takes a clear understanding of a situation to avoid reacting, to exercise physical and verbal restraint.

Speak little and speak softly, aware of the pointlessness of unnecessary words.

We spend so much time talking about third parties—which is totally useless speech. Gossip, backbiting, and undermining are useless, as is harsh and abusive language.

The key to listening deeply is to stay in touch with the messages coming to you from your body, heart, and open mind.

[S]ilence is as full of potential wisdom and wit as the unhewn marble of great sculpture. (Aldous Huxley)

In learning to listen both outwardly and inwardly before you speak, you begin to appreciate the path with heart.

Use awareness to resist the urge to talk about others—and begin to live in the present moment with whoever is with you and no one else.

Cultivating wise speech asks you to restrain the inclinations in your heart and mind that express themselves as unwise speech.

Love means little if your major way of expressing it is to pressure others to conform to your views of how they should be or what they should do.

When in doubt, tell the truth. (Mark Twain)

Acknowledge that the contents of your thoughts are not facts. You can shape your world through the wisdom of mindful awareness and insight.

Express gentleness to all things, and just relax.

You can learn to become resilient by intercepting your reactions to smaller, everyday irritations.

Harsh language that is habitual, like profanity, is mindless. You can unlearn this habit. When you become aware of what you are saying and want to change it, you can.

Mindful encouragement restores your intuitive wisdom so that you know how to respond appropriately.

Resist the temptation to judge and talk about others.

Speech causes us emotional pain only when we let it arouse us.

Grant me the serenity to accept the things I cannot change, the courage to change the things I can, and the wisdom to know the difference. (Serenity Prayer)

In the middle of an argument, when you find yourself about to unleash a verbal weapon against someone, ask yourself, "Do I really want to cause permanent harm to this relationship?"

Speak in a way that fosters dignity, respect, and simplicity.

Refraining from idle chatter is a practice of mindfulness that cultivates simplicity.

It can be helpful in setting the tone of a meeting to open with a spoken agreement that the participants will respect each other's words and be open to the views of others.

Anger quickly spreads through insensitive comments, unhelpful criticism, and continuous complaining. The more you do this, the more others pass it on, and the more damage is done.

Follow your breath while carrying on a conversation by breathing long, light, even breaths. Follow your breath while listening to someone's words and to your own replies.

Be willing to listen for the answer. You have to get still enough to hear it. Pay attention and be fully conscious.

Arguing is useless. To uproot the anger that starts an argument, name it and give it space. Shine the light of awareness on it and it loses its power over you. Vow to be mindful of your speech.

Remember that a word is an action.

Allow silence by deliberately interrupting your conversations and activities with a mindfulness bell.

All actions have consequences. When someone's actions are unthoughtful, you may react in a mean way. When you are mean-spirited or harmful, you will experience guilt, confusion, and regret.

Express love by listening.

When you consistently interrupt, it is likely that your preoccupation with status or self is rearing its ugly head.

Your karma is made by thought, speech, and actions. If an ugly or unhelpful thought arises, take care that it does not turn into speech or action. Make good and wise choices.

Practice talking with your eyes closed, as if going somewhere inside to verbalize.

A voice rooted in wisdom treasures truthfulness, respect, and compassion. Is it true? Is it useful? Practicing these principles fosters increased sensitivity.

Why do you talk so much when you should be doing something useful? Do something useful in silence with a relaxed mind.

When inner and outer dialogues are going on, they hide loneliness, keep us from being bored or feeling afraid, and fill up all the space that is empty or scared. You can only grow when things get quieter and you really see.

Interrupt, or disengage from, the momentum of an aggressive communication.

Many of us carry the guilt of something we have said or done that we think we can't rectify. But you can speak to that person, see her smiling to you, and heal the suffering of the past.

Wisdom is revealed through action, not talk.

When you are around family, be completely present. The greatest gift you can offer anyone is your true presence.

Silence offers us and those around us the spaciousness needed to speak more skillfully. Then, when you do speak, your compassionate, loving self can emerge.

Sometimes silence may be the best course.

Try this approach with your not-so-favorite people: Listen to them from the standpoint that there is something to learn from them. You may grow to appreciate these various perspectives.

Psychological disengagement from a bully is more important than attempting to make him see the light.

Cultivate mindfulness to recognize and confront ill will. Otherwise, ill will can become harsh speech.

Although it can be comforting to know that others have had and survived a bad experience, most people cannot derive comfort from hearing your experience or the supposed silver lining.

Let thy speech be short, comprehending much in few words. (Apocrypha, Ecclesiasticus)

Listening well under stress is hard because your thinking turns inward. Stepping back to determine where these emotions are coming from helps loosen their grip on the psyche.

When you do not want others to think you are out of control, you use words to control what others do.

Make amends for thoughts, words, and actions you recognize as wrong.

Whatever words we utter should be chosen with care, for people will hear them and be influenced by them for good or ill. (Buddha)

The pen is mightier than the sword. (Edward G. Bulwer-Lytton)

Gossip is the infliction of suffering from a distance that appears to protect you.

When your position is based on logic and sound reasoning, you can speak gently and quietly.

Talk heart-to-heart with someone who needs it.

Practice telling and hearing the truth.

Nonviolent thoughts are as important as nonviolent words; let your negative thoughts go.

The Buddha urged that we abstain from speaking negatively.

As mindfulness gets sharper, you begin to be aware before talking. The intention to speak arises and you are mindful of it.

Attend to your speech and be sensitive to the accuracy of the message and the possible interpretations that could be derived from it.

By being a good listener, you promote the good health of others, allowing them to reduce their stress and empowering them to solve their own dilemmas.

Becoming aware of every body sensation, sound, and mood as it unfolds in the moment helps you control attention and better face troubling thoughts.

Endure anger or sadness and let it pass without ruminating on it or trying to change the feeling.

Practice conscious communication, sitting in silence or taking three deep breaths before making a call, going into a meeting, or writing an important e-mail.

When angry count to ten before you speak.
   If very angry, count to one hundred.
   (Thomas Jefferson)

Communicate unconditional love.

Practice putting your own feelings and
   judgments aside when you listen to others.

Be easy to speak to, gentle and not proud.

Better than a thousand words mindlessly
   spoken is one word of truth that helps
   bring peace to the listener. (Buddha)

Let your conversations and interactions with
   people throughout the day become
   opportunities to practice deep listening
   and mindful speaking.

Write a love poem or letter from the bottom
   of your heart.

Speech is a mirror of the soul: as a man
speaks, so is he. (Publilius Syrus)

When we hear so much speech that causes
craving, insecurity, and anger, we get
accustomed to speaking that way. Truthful,
loving speech is something we need to
train ourselves in.

Keep quiet if you can't say anything nice.

To meditate is to listen with a receptive
heart.

There needs to be mindfulness and
skillfulness on the part of both speaker
and listener.

Speaking harshly is a sign of weakness, not
strength.

Loving, receptive silence invites the
confidence and trust of others.

True eloquence consists in saying all that should be said, and that only. (La Rochefoucauld)

When you gossip, you sacrifice sensitivity, kindness, and compassion.

If silence is uncomfortable or threatening, you may feel you must fill it with words.

There is a big difference between hearing someone and listening to someone.

Verbal abuse that is intended to hurt another person might have immediate negative karmic effect.

We need a reason to speak, but none to keep silent. (Pierre Nicole)

To listen before you speak is the heart of wise and simple communication.

There is probably nothing you could do that would have a more immediate positive effect on your life and on those around you than becoming more mindful of the words you speak.

Sometimes the best way to feel your feelings or think your thoughts is to sit in silence. You are less distracted and can be more fully aware of the essence of your feelings and thoughts.

As you look at feelings and thoughts more deeply, you give them space. Sitting in silence is full of potential wisdom.

Feeling uncomfortable or threatened by silence is no excuse for filling all your time with thoughts and words.

During discussions of charged or touchy issues, be mindful of the words you are using for signs of defensiveness, argumentativeness, and the urge to get away.

If an angry driver wants to get by you, let him. Say "After you." Flow with the traffic instead of fighting with it.

Put aside your point of view and get into what the other person is expressing.

By opening your mind and softening your heart, you can use disappointment and the other ups and downs of your life as stepping stones toward reality instead of away from it.

By practicing mindful speech, you break the habit of exaggerating and suppressing and cut the root of the toxic emotions they trigger.

Not judging or suppressing your emotional
reactions, but instead coming back to the
breath, gives you distance from thoughts,
making it easier to respond calmly.

Breathing before you speak solves many
problems.

When you are angry, do not be centered on
the person who has aroused the anger. Let
her be on the periphery. Feel the wound
and be grateful to the other person for
helping you recognize this.

Open up, let go of words, stay present in
your body, and feel the energy in your
heart. When your mind gets hooked by an
interpretation, touch that lightly and let it
go.

It is helpful to stop for a moment before you
speak to make certain that what you are
about to say is skillful or healing.

Whenever the phone rings, you can hear it as a bell of mindfulness and stop whatever you're doing. Instead of rushing to answer the phone, you can breathe in and out with awareness.

Before answering the phone or an e-mail, make sure you're truly present. Recognize any feelings of stress or irritation you may have or any feeling that you're being interrupted.

When you get attached or angry, don't react or speak. Remain mum and unmoved, like a tree.

Learn to recognize a contentious communication, then stop and let go instead of pushing forward into the danger zone. Be curious about what happens when communication shuts down.

In the space of a pause, you can learn to replace defensive habits with a more realistic way of responding when a problem arises.

You may accuse someone of not hearing you when, in truth, they heard you perfectly but they simply do not agree. Remember that others are entitled to their views just as you are entitled to yours.

As a mindful listener, you strive to relate to the needs—positive or negative—of the speaker. If this seems difficult, imagine how you would like people to respond to you in a similar situation.

Get up and talk to someone; don't yell across rooms or to other floors.

You can use your speech patterns to help you communicate with others in a more considered, conscious way. Or you can be careless and create trouble with your words.

The more you practice mindfulness, the more you'll see things you can do to change your work environment in a positive way.

The question is: Is it worth saying?

Judgmental words and self-righteous tones do not help any situation.

Express your most positive thoughts and feelings. Tell others that you care about them.

Use words to nourish and support loved ones.

During an argument, you may want to be hurtful. When this happens, reclaim the problem as your own and do not blame others. Apologize. Take care of your own emotional needs.

Nature, which gave us two eyes to see, and two ears to hear, has given us but one tongue to speak. (Jonathan Swift)

Gentleness reconnects you with the strength of your natural heart by opening you up to the sadness of feeling powerless when you reach your limits.

Cultivate a voice that is easy to listen to.

In practicing mindfulness, you can begin to understand and discover the power of speech.

Center and collect yourself each time you begin an e-mail. Be mindful of all your words. Be conscious of your tone and whether you are saying what you really want to say.

Right Speech is not indulging in lies, gossip, or other thoughtless talk.

Ask yourself whether what you are about to say or do will be useful.

Listen to what other people want without reacting, objecting, arguing, fighting, or resisting.

What you read and watch can help you heal, so be thoughtful about what you consume.

Speech also reflects the credibility of the speaker; you are often measured by the way and manner in which you speak.

Say only what is true, speak in ways that promote harmony among people, use a pleasing tone of voice, and speak mindfully in order that your speech is useful and purposeful.

Life has much to do with verbalization—talking, thinking, reading, writing. We worship language and are addicted to it.

Most of the time, we are concerned not with what the other person is saying but with our response to it.

Speak slowly, calmly, quietly, clearly, and with confidence.

You can skillfully adapt to circumstances beyond your control using positivity to counter the habit of angry reaction.

Deep listening means listening with your entire being.

Have you ever wanted to say something you considered important and then did not have the courage to say it? Try saying it next time.

Try listening to yourself so you can hear how you sound from a different perspective, as if being outside of yourself, like an objective listener.

[L]anguage, the most valuable single possession of the human race. (Charles F. Hockett)

When your mind is chattering away, it is not looking. Try watching yourself in silence. You need to watch, understand, and deal with your anger, desire, and ignorance as they occur.

To understand the mind, you have to pay attention with an uncluttered, silent mind. Only when you cease to be involved with your emotions can the peaceful nature of your mind emerge.

Before I speak, I have something important to say. (Groucho Marx)

Words have the power to inspire, encourage, comfort, and uplift.

Use positive self-talk from morning until bedtime.

Do you speak at the right time? Do you speak factually? Do you speak gently? Do you speak with words that will be of benefit? Do you speak with a kind heart?

The capacity for verbal expression has been regarded as the distinguishing mark of the human species. Appreciate the need to make this capacity a means for human excellence.

Choose the right moment to open your mouth.

Don't use your words to control or manipulate others.

The residues of hurtful words sift down into emotional memory to cast long shadows over the inner landscape of your mind.

You have a much better chance of being heard when you speak calmly and patiently.

Ask yourself, Am I resisting the temptation to judge and talk about others?

Be as aware as possible of your thoughts and emotions to prevent harsh speech. When you are aware, you can see the impulse to be cruel, especially when you are preoccupied or frustrated.

A person is not good or bad for one thing that she says.

When you sit and breathe mindfully, your mind and body finally get to communicate and come together.

Wise men speak because they have something to say; fools because they have to say something. (Plato)

Unless you are mindful and know what you are saying, you should keep quiet and try to find out what you are thinking.

Instead of lashing out at people who offend you, work to turn an unpleasant situation into an opportunity to benefit all involved.

However many holy words you read, however many you speak, what good will they do you if you do not act on them? (Buddha)

Most people agree that they would rather be interrupted than have someone pretend that they are listening.

We fill up space, the void of our fear and anxiety, with words. Sometimes we even talk to ourselves. To eliminate such unskillful states, simply be aware in the moment.

When it is your turn to speak, indicate that you have carefully considered the other person's message by making a connection between her interests and yours.

If you are the one responsible for inciting an argument, mindfulness may give you the courage to explore your internal conflicts.

When you are frustrated, you can intervene before you get angry. When there is nothing to actually be done, you can intervene and remind yourself not to add bitterness to frustration.

Meditation allows your mind to hear with less distortion new ideas and points of view. Practice it, and you will notice that you are less anxious when hearing ideas that differ from your point of view.

Meditation increases your ability to concentrate more deeply and longer, and you can better focus your attention on getting and retaining messages from others.

What is speech that is not harsh? It can be firm, pointed, or intense. It can confront mistreatment or injustice. It can acknowledge anger.

When you listen with compassion, you can understand things that you wouldn't be able to understand if you were full of anger.

Respond to aggression with compassion.

When someone you love says something that feels critical or dismissive, you suffer deeply. Remember this and change how you speak to others.

The tools that are supposed to save us time can take more of it. Those created to help us communicate can actually lead to less genuine, less purposeful communication.

Learn to see every instance of harm as an opportunity, as something you can use to benefit yourself and others.

Let thy speech be better than silence, or be silent. (Dionysius the Elder)

Look for the golden nugget or the seed of opportunity for growth hidden deep within a stressful listening situation.

Could what you are complaining about be a blessing? Are you mistakenly viewing as a weed something that actually is a great treasure, and vice versa?

Mindfulness requires letting go of judgment, returning to awareness. This helps you notice whether the thought you just produced is healthy or unhealthy, compassionate or unkind.

He's my friend that speaks well of me behind my back. (Thomas Fuller)

Occasionally saying out loud the kind thoughts you are thinking can help make a relationship more intimate. Being yourself can be a valuable way to deepen relationships.

When you are angry or upset about something that someone did, if you pause and take three breaths, you will discover other options and react in a better way, without anger.

Harsh language can produce aversion in those to whom it is directed. When the objects of such language do not have the power to withdraw, they can be caused deep suffering.

Remember that kids take note of everything adults do and say.

Ask, listen, and hear to determine the wants and needs of others.

Take advantage of all the opportunities to keep your mouth shut.

Opening your heart and mind, fully hear what others tell you so that you may nourish understanding and strengthen the connection between you.

A silent lunch break can go a long way in helping you get in touch with inner peace.

To alter a core belief, all you really have to do is see it, be aware of it. If you truly see a core belief for what it is, even when it tries to run its story, you can't quite buy into it anymore.

Practicing the precepts of asking yourself, "Is it true? Is it useful?" fosters increased sensitivity. You become attuned to the subtleties of truth and falsehood.

Getting to know your personal barriers and the energy you waste trying to reinforce them is a big step in becoming a better listener.

Silence is one of the most powerful response modes, but—regrettably—the least practiced.

Always be truthful, especially with a child.

Think about what it means to take a vow of silence for a short period of time. You would commune only with yourself and rest your mind.

Cultivate virtue by what you read, listen to, and watch.

Love is the ultimate way to transform people, even those who are full of hatred. Love is the only answer to hatred. Hatred never ceases by hatred. By love alone it is healed.

Let your words reflect the person you want to be rather than a reactive, flippant individual.

Everything you say can express your spiritual nature.

You begin to realize that your aggressive patterns of speech spill out into the world from inner-bully voices within your own mind. Seeing this, compassionate insight begins to dawn.

Talk only when necessary. Value silence.

There is no sickness worse / For me than words that to be kind must lie. (Aeschylus)

We are so conditioned to relating to others in adversarial terms that we seldom think of how futile that is as a way of living.

[I]t is impossible to speak in such a way that you cannot be misunderstood. (Karl Popper)

Setting others against each other can be a way of making yourself feel powerful, but it carries a lot of negative energy. Do you sometimes join in with gossiping or criticism to feel part of a group?

Begin any communication in a friendly way.

Uneasiness with silence of any kind is a major reason why so many of us have trouble listening.

Men are born with two eyes, but with one tongue, in order that they should see twice as much as they say. (Charles Caleb Colton)

Respond to fear by offering protection.

To practice responding mindfully, you need to gently pop the bubbles of past and future, tune in to the present moment, and listen for clues about what needs to be done next.

A steady stream of internal focusing blocks your ability to listen.

To be mindful and honest makes your mind quieter and more open, your heart happier and more peaceful.

Hold everything in until you have figured out how to say it in a useful way.

Because the effects of wrong speech may not be as immediately evident as the effects of bodily actions, the impact of wrong speech is sometimes overlooked.

Think about how you would prefer to have a conversation. When you practice mindful speech and deep listening, you can make conversations deeper, more meaningful, and more satisfying.

When you write an e-mail or a letter that is full of understanding and compassion, you are nourishing yourself during the time you write it.

When you are shaken by feelings of anger, hurt, or resentment, your speech takes on a momentum or life of its own. You speak bitterly, recounting every detail of the hurt.

Practice listening; you don't learn anything new when you are speaking.

The best antidote to anger is loving-kindness. Realize that only someone who is unhappy will hurt someone else. Hurtful people cannot be happy, and you should feel compassion, not anger, toward them.

Much is lost in electronic communication because the communicators "hear" the information differently. People tend to believe they communicate more effectively than they actually do.

He that would live in peace and at ease, / Must not speak all he knows, nor judge all he sees. (Benjamin Franklin)

"Swallow the words" is wise advice if it guides you to deeper listening and attunement.

How many of us have endured silences that are hostile, a withdrawal of love, or an expression of judgment?

A misperception can happen in a moment and you get caught by it. So anything you say or do based on that perception can be dangerous. Sometimes it is better not to say or do anything.

When you are not sure of the truth, you do not have to speak.

Mindfulness practice is the foundation of your love. You cannot love properly and deeply without mindfulness.

Whenever possible, it is always a good idea to take a couple of days to carefully notice the intentions that motivate your comments, opinions, and responses to hunches and events.

To transform aggressive speech, interrupt the story lines that arise in your conversations to support your beliefs and opinions.

Instead of hanging up on a telemarketer, just say, "I am not interested, but thank you for calling."

The best approach is to simply stop for a moment, breathe, and become aware of precisely what is taking place. You will act more skillfully, appropriately, and with consideration.

If you constantly subject someone to anger, she will look for a chance to hurt you. Even your family, friends, and partners will lose affection for you if you constantly blow up at them.

When it is difficult to make a decision, pause before acting. Ask yourself, Is this action skillful and wholesome? If the action will cause harm to yourself or someone else, do not do it.

Temper your anger. Arguing is useless.

A person may present you with what he thinks is a situation that deserves an immediate response. He wants you to be as stressed as he is. Carefully consider how to respond.

Cultivate the art of never complaining.

After a misunderstanding, be the first to say you are sorry.

Respond to grief with comfort.

Develop the ability to wait and to listen.

Rule 1: Be cautious, careful, and when in doubt, keep your mouth shut. Rule 2: When tempted to say something, take a deep breath and refer to Rule 1. (Lance Ito)

Do call to tell your family if you are delayed or your plans change.

With your words you confirm to the world, sometimes hundreds of times every day, what you think is important. Your words have power.

All the gestures or words we exchange with each other originate from a deep human longing for connection, for acknowledgment and appreciation.

Karma means watching your body, watching your mouth, and watching your mind.

Silence is the element in which great things fashion themselves together, that at length they may emerge, full-formed and majestic, into the daylight of Life, which they are henceforth to rule. (Maurice Maeterlinck)

When you produce a thought that carries suspicion, anger, fear, or irritation, that thought is not nourishing to you or to the other person.

You can use words that will nourish yourself and nourish another person.

Use words with the greatest care.

Try being aware of the other person you have to talk to in a sensitive situation. Ground yourself in breathing and see the situation as a whole, without speaking out of fear.

Nothing can help or hurt you as much as the thoughts you carry in your head. You can often balance hatred or anger by developing thoughts of compassion and forgiveness.

Silence can be a way of demonstrating love.

Slander is attempting to build oneself up by tearing another person down.

By diminishing the value of silence, publicity has also diminished that of language. The two are inseparable: knowing how to speak has always meant knowing how to keep silent, knowing that there are times when one should say nothing. (Octavio Paz)

The Buddha emphasized the importance of Right Speech when he included it as a distinct part of the path to awakening.

When you begin to understand the role of your words in a conflict, you will start to feel relief.

Study the wrong speech in your life; look at the moments when you use it. Do not judge your wrong speech, but try to understand and see what is going on when you engage in it.

A little trick to help with speaking: hear twice before you speak once.

Sometimes you can tell the story of someone else whose situation is similar to the person you are speaking to, so that he can understand the idea.

The ear is a door; it allows. Listening to nature, traffic, or music—just listening, doing nothing—great silence comes in and great peace starts coming to you.

Express thanks often.

Write with confidence, relaxed and happy. At the end, see yourself feeling extremely pleased with what you have done and confident that you have written with quality.

Most people would rather talk than listen.

You can comment on just about anything online—items, videos, blogs, podcasts, articles, social media. You can even comment on comments. The challenge is knowing when *not* to comment.

You have to have the capacity to say things calmly. Don't get irritated too easily. Don't let sour or bitter speech leave your mouth. Get back a capacity for speaking with kindness.

Turn toward meditation. Know there is nothing to seek but also know that there is nothing to say. Keep your mouth closed.

It's the people we care most about who trigger our greatest suffering.

Right Speech is refraining from harmful speech and also generating kind speech.

Before speaking, notice what motivates your words.

Do you sometimes use words to distance yourself from others and protect your true feelings?

Who do you most enjoy listening to? What is it about their talk (or tone) that makes it welcome?

Write a note of appreciation to one of your favorite teachers or mentors about the difference she made in your life.

Saying too much is just as bad as saying too little.

The way you think about your work and your work relationships affects how you communicate in your work environment.

A person who talks with equal vivacity on every subject, excites no interest in any. Repose is as necessary in conversation as in a picture. (William Hazlitt)

The most common drama is cruel comments. It is not hard to be cruel with the truth and it is not helpful, either.

Quarrels would not last long if the fault was only on one side. (La Rochefoucauld)

Gossip is an evil thing by nature, she's a light weight to lift up, / oh very easy, but heavy to carry, and hard to put down again. (Hesiod)

Mindfulness makes you more resilient when everyday crises occur. You might remember how unrealistic it is to depend on others' seeing or hearing you accurately.

In silence, start to hear your own true voice.

Imagine yourself sitting in a very quiet place. You feel the wisdom building up inside you. You are learning the wisdom of silence. You stop trying to speak and you just sit, becoming wiser.

Every time we choose the good action or response, the decent, the valuable, it builds, incrementally, to renewal, resurrection, the place of newness, freedom, justice. (Anne Lamott)

If one cannot say something useful, one should keep Noble Silence.

Ask yourself: Does something really have to be said?

To create an unfavorable impression, it is not necessary that certain things should be true, but that they have been said. (William Hazlitt)

If you can keep your compassion alive, the seeds of anger and judgment in your heart will not be watered and spring up.

Mean what you say.

Excuse yourself from people-bashing sessions at the outset and you will be on your way to eliminating a major block to mindful listening.

One falsehood spoils a thousand truths.
(Ashanti proverb)

You always have time for at least one in-breath and out-breath before you pick up the phone or before you press "Send" on a text or e-mail.

The fourth aspect of Right Speech is to refrain from speech that's violent, condemning, abusive, humiliating, accusing, or judgmental.

When you start practicing mindful communication, you realize how many of your emotional dramas are self-created.

Life is hard enough without having an ongoing soap opera in your mind to deal with. But your thoughts generate all kinds of stories that stir up intense reactions within you.

Express your positive feelings, no matter how trivial they seem.

Try a period of no speech, no radio, no television, no newspaper, no books, and no notes, notebooks, or recording devices for a period of time. It is quieting for the heart, mind, energy, and mouth.

Know that not everything needs to be said.

Who have you not said something to that you really need to? Think about this and see what stops you from saying it.

Have control over your thoughts to have control over your speech.

Write a note that says "I need you."

Getting angry at someone will never make you feel better in the long term.

Part of being awake is slowing down enough to notice what you say and do. Make it your way of life to stay awake, slow down, and notice.

To be brief is almost a condition of being inspired. (George Santayana)

Allow empathy to wake you up and give you a tender heart.

Do not think that because you are suffering you can speak harshly, retaliate, or punish others. Breathe in and remember your Buddha nature, your capacity for calm and compassion.

The next time your cell phone rings while you are driving or spending time with a friend, look at your reaction. Sense not knowing and wanting to know. Where is your attention most needed at this time?

Gossiping is not being in the present moment. If you are not in the present moment, you are not in touch with reality.

Sometimes workplace communication can seem so difficult, but one mindful breath already begins to make it easier.

If you learn how to listen, then you will learn how to speak.

It's helpful to remember at the beginning of every communication with another person that there is a Buddha inside each of us.

If you begin balancing out negative self-talk with positive self-talk, it may be easier for you to vocalize positive comments about others.

When someone insults you, be intelligent enough to see that the other person suffers from his own words and anger. Do not return the sarcasm or slander, but practice patience instead.

An insult becomes yours only if you choose to accept and engage it. An insult can only come from within, not from a situation.

Patience and forbearance in the face of anger are the hardest practices.

After you sit with mindful awareness and calm your anger, you can look deeply into the root of that anger. Does it come from a wrong perception or a habitual way of responding?

Instead of anger, conceive of every pain as something that will make you better able to deal with any future pain. So, bearing such a pain will seem like an achievement.

The toxic patterns in your communication can be traced back to a false system of trying to protect yourself from fear and pain.

You cannot possess the people you love, or hold on to moments of joy. Realizing this, emotional reactions become more mature and you learn to tolerate the feeling of being misunderstood.

When you have a habit of talking too much and your speech does not serve you or the people you are talking to well, make a conscious effort to restrain yourself.

So much time in our lives is spent talking, discussing, and gossiping about unimportant or irrelevant things that it does not serve us or the people we are talking to in a positive way.

A good listener encourages the speaker to continue developing her idea through a combination of silence, good eye contact, and verbal support.

When someone is yelling at you, keep your voice soft and steady, just like your breath. This voice response can be very helpful in quieting the other person's voice.

Plan days with no conversation, only contemplation.

Everything that goes wrong starts with speech.

Essays

Anger

Anger is considered a "normal" emotion, but it is important to deal with it in a positive way. If you allow some space for it, you will feel differently and perhaps you will actively (rather than reactively) decide what to do with it. Instead of exploding, maybe you can express anger in a constructive way without hurting anyone. You cannot sweep anger under the carpet. You must face it.

Anger is a by-product of dealing with people. It is natural to sometimes feel anger toward a person, but it is important that you understand the anger. First you must study yourself and the situations you may experience as especially difficult. By identifying the behaviors that get to you the most, you can then mentally practice detaching from the feeling of anger.

Part of studying yourself means understanding your temperament. Do you get easily frustrated? Are you impatient? After you begin to understand your temperament, work toward developing nonreactiveness. One of the best things you can teach yourself is to walk away or start counting or take deep breaths. Most situations turn out better if you do not lash out but, rather, pause and consider whether to react at all, and if so, how to do it effectively. A good way to develop nonreactiveness is to watch the anger rise, then watch it fall.

Develop a flexibility of emotional response. In the face of anger, for example, practice generating compassion toward yourself and others. A few moments of breathing deeply and counting will help you slow down and defuse your temper. Once you are calm, you can clearly express your frustration or upset in an assertive, nonconfrontational way. State your concerns and needs directly without hurting others or trying to control them. Remind yourself that anger won't fix anything, and might only make it worse.

Think before you speak. In the heat of the moment it's easy to say something you'll later regret. Take a few moments to collect your thoughts before saying anything—and allow others involved in the situation to do the same.

Barbara Ann Kipfer

Arguing and Fighting

Discontent may fuel our doing the most absurd things in order to change what we believe to be the cause. We argue, trying to change the people we live with. Why? Because we are not content. But such actions will never bring contentment. That can only be done through patient, persevering effort plus insight. During discussions of charged or touchy issues, be mindful of the words you are using, keeping an eye out for signs of defensiveness, argumentativeness, and the urge to get away.

To uproot the confusion that starts an argument or to get rid of anger or restlessness, just acknowledge the state of mind, naming it and giving it space. If you shine the light of awareness on it, it loses its power over you.

One approach is to treat the seed of an argument as if it is a gift, the opportunity to learn. The first thing you learn is that you started the argument or entered into the argument because you are clinging to something you want. You want something to be different than it is, you have expectations, you want something to change or to stay the same and whatever it is is not happening the way you want it to. If you pause for a moment and think before starting or entering into an argument, you may be able to identify what you are clinging to. This is a moment of great learning. This "gift" may be all you need to stop the communication from being negative and turn it around into something that also benefits the other party.

Respect is a necessary condition for the resolution of arguments or fights. Most arguments and fights are an absurd waste of time and effort and the cause of misery. Aggression is an ineffective way to handle problems. So the first step is to have both sides state their positions clearly and recognize the point of view and demands of the other side. This is respect. Resolving an argument or fight by way of careful listening and mutual respect is the most efficient and elegant way to settle a disagreement.

Asking for What You Want or Need

All people, babies to adults, need warmth—psychological and physical. We need to be touched and cuddled. We need someone to talk to, someone who knows and appreciates us, someone who cares about us. You must ask for what you want, unless you can give yourself what you want or need—or unless you let go of wanting, which takes practice and time. But, otherwise, you have to ask. Human beings are interconnected and interdependent, but we cannot read each other's minds. Only you can express when you want or need something from another person. When you ask for what you want, the answer may be no. If you don't ask, the answer is always no.

It is not a sign of weakness to assert and ask for what you want or need. Yes, you have to be prepared for rejection or someone to insensitively blow off what you ask for. But with practice, especially with loved ones who may not be used to your honestly asking for what you want, you will see that you start getting positive responses. Ask politely and directly for what you want. You will get nowhere by raising your voice or whining.

If you need to talk, you ask for a time to talk. If you need to get out of the house—to have a date with your partner, for example— then simply ask. Even if you need a day alone, however selfish it may seem, it is something you should ask for. These things may rejuvenate you, make you feel more appreciative of your life, make you happier.

Since asking for what you want or need frequently involves loved ones, it is important to note that asking for what you want or need may reduce the number of arguments you have with them. If the request is reasonable and you have taken into account the timing of the request, many loved ones will be eager to give you what you want or need. They will experience a sense of happiness because they are able to make you happy or satisfied. You will also experience more happiness as this becomes a habit. With all parties asking for what they want or need, relationships can improve and love grows. In return, you need to also respond positively to other people's requests as often as you can.

Being Present

See the perfectness of the present moment in every ordinary moment, in every hard moment, in every good moment. Appreciate, respond, and sense the "bloom" of each moment. Dwelling in the present moment, know that this is a wonderful moment.

Bring yourself back into the present moment by becoming mindful of objects and events that are arising. Know you are breathing in. Know you are breathing out. Be aware of the hair on your head. Be aware of the soles of your feet. Dwell in the present moment. Be aware that this is the only moment when you are alive.

When you are standing there impatiently trying to get the toaster to work faster, wake up! Breathe, smile, and settle into the present moment. During the three minutes that the toaster is doing its thing, just breathe and calm yourself. Waiting for the toast is an opportunity for you to experience peace.

Become aware of other opportunities that arise for you to meditate on the present moment. The more you practice it, the better you will get. You will reach a point where you love being in each and every moment.

Bullying

We think of bullying mainly in the context of kids. Children can be very unkind because of how they are treated at home, because of what they read and see in the media, and because they are in their formative years and are working on building self-esteem and self-confidence. It's a busy, fast, tough world for kids growing up. And there are so many venues in which bullying can take place, including venues like text messaging and social media that did not exist for the parents of these children when they were growing up.

Children can use kindness to defuse a bullying episode. But in a dangerous situation where kindness will not have an effect, kids should know how to quickly remove themselves from the situation. In this case, the child does not respond and just walks away.

Educating kids and ourselves to "see" bullying as a form of suffering is insightful. It teaches that bullies are hurting and angry, and need our compassion more than our criticism. It is important to remember that no one is born wanting to be a bully. They learned it and they can unlearn it.

When you sense that others are being treated unfairly, take carefully considered action. Bullying exists in every milieu of life, and it takes a brave soul to stand up to the bully, or to expose injustice to those with the power to act. But you owe it to your values not to be a passive bystander. We can strengthen our children's and our own abilities to be strong from the inside out.

Children

Mothers and fathers who are calm and happy bring affection and a sense of caring into the lives of their children, thereby transforming society into something more compassionate and peaceful. If we as parents listen and speak mindfully, our children will learn to do the same. Soft words help children flourish and grow up with a positive feeling of self-worth.

If you take care of your own practice, children in your life will learn from the kindness and clarity you exemplify. Our children love respect; they want respect for their needs and fears.

It's easy to forget that children have their own opinions. Include them in discussions on family matters. Even if you don't agree with their suggestions, you can thank them for their contribution and show them that you value their views.

Children, especially very young ones, can help us enter into beginner's mind—that state before concepts, conditioning, and defenses insulate us from experiencing directly. Try seeing children as your teachers. Observe them in silence sometimes. Listen more carefully to them. Be fully present and available and open.

Commenting and Opinion

A major part of wrong speech is commenting. If you vowed not to speak about any person— present or not present, even if the comment was favorable—you would find more than 90 percent of your speech eliminated!

The most common problem is cruel comments. Usually, angry comments by someone are requests for more attention. It is easy to be cruel, and it is not helpful. When you are subjected to others' mean comments, you can usually end the situation by listening—really listening—rather than reacting. When you are the one constantly commenting on what others are doing, saying, and so on, you need to address this aspect of wrong speech. Comments, if made at all, should be positive, useful, and timely. If you are open and present, attentive to the moment, with practice this will become easy.

Our suffering is generated from within our own minds. Fixed opinions make us feel defensive and anxious; cravings make us feel frustrated and dissatisfied; dislikes and hates make us feel irritable and tormented. The judging mind has an opinion about everything.

Experiment with how it feels to not be attached to opinions. For a day, resolve to let go of judgments and conclusions. Recognize when your point of view is not resting on an actual experience but is simply an opinion. Learning to listen inwardly, you learn to pause before assuming that any of your conclusions or opinions are absolutely true. Stop frantically trying to have an opinion about what is going on and simply say, "I don't know."

Complaining

If you traced the evolution of a complaint, it would likely look something like this: unmet expectations lead to dissatisfaction, which leads to a complaint, which lead to attempts to resolve the complaint, which fail, leading to more complaining, which leads to frustration, which leads to threats if things don't change, which lead to ultimatums, which finally lead to consequences. Complaining is an ineffective way of dealing with suffering.

Complaint is the by-product of an untamed mind. Narrowing your mind with complaint is unpleasant and claustrophobic. Complaint is frustrating and painful. Resistance, moping, complaining, and whining are insidious and self-destructive. Negativity takes its toll, unbalancing your life.

Use your willpower to catch every negative thought that passes through your mind. If you are complaining about the weather or disturbed or bothered by anything or anyone, catch those negative thoughts. See them, don't judge them, then let them go. Neutralize a negative thought by substituting a positive one for it. Study, contemplate, and remember spiritual teachings that can help your mind go beyond temporary situations in which those negative thoughts arise.

Try reframing how you respond when difficult outer events come up. If you complain, what will that do? It is better to let go than to dwell on something or complain about it, especially when you know it will change, just like everything else in life.

Conversation

Practice complete focus in conversation. This means not only listening well but also being willing to openly share your own thoughts, experiences, and emotions when appropriate. In your conversations, you may be so intent on getting your messages across that you are not really paying attention to what other people are trying to say. You are waiting for them to stop speaking so you can say what is on your mind.

Relish the pauses and also trust the flow within the conversation. Make a conscious effort to relax your breathing during the conversation and focus on listening to the other person and having control of what you are saying.

Follow your breath while carrying on a conversation by breathing long, light, even breaths. Follow your breath while listening to a friend's words and to your own replies. Let your conversations and interactions with people throughout the day become opportunities to practice deep listening and mindful speaking. Mindfulness can help make your conversations deeper, more meaningful, more satisfying.

Criticism

Criticism—chiding yourself, judging some-body else, thinking you need to change, fix, or improve something—is a problem. It is a bad habit that can be broken by increasing awareness.

You can become aware that you con-stantly react to stimuli and this leads you to understand your motivation. Your motive for criticizing is to get a result, to change things. The moment you are not looking for a result—not looking to criticize, to evaluate, to conclude—then you can perceive this reacting and release yourself from it. You can stop being critical because you let go of trying to control things. You do this to improve your life as well as those of others.

Accept criticism directed toward you whether it is justified or not. When we're crit-icized, we naturally want to justify ourselves, but this isn't always necessary, and often it does more harm than good. Usually people engage in negativity and excessive criticism out of feelings of jealousy, anger, or low self-esteem.

And self-criticism? Learn from your mistakes, but don't berate yourself for them. If you allow your inner critic to voice its opinions too loudly and too often, you'll find that your ability to face new challenges diminishes. Take your constructive inner criticism on board, then move on.

Dating

Your ability to be in the present moment, not rehashing the past (*What did I say last night?*) or plotting out the future (*When she walks in, I will start talking about X or Y*), will be appreciated by the person you are dating. Practicing staying in the present moment means you will be listening when the other person is talking and it also means you will be paying attention to what you say before and as you say it. By doing this, you will be giving the gift of kindness.

You can let yourself be more open and natural so that you know better who you are and what you want. You can relax, smile at your fears, and develop the courage to be authentic and honest in what you communicate. This will allow you to be seen and loved for who you are instead of hiding, pushing others away, or putting on a false façade. As you feel more secure, you will worry less about what others think or how they respond to you and this will bring greater intimacy in relationships. You will communicate with compassion, understanding, and love.

In dating, remember there is a circular relationship between your ability to know and love another and your ability to know and love yourself. Be where you are. Pay attention to the person you're with instead of comparing her to an ideal in your mind.

E-mailing

You know how much e-mail you get, and how much you send. You likely have a memory of a hurtful e-mail that was sent to you, or one you sent that was hurtful or misunderstood. There's no getting around the importance of carefully writing your e-mails and responding mindfully to the ones you receive.

Some people want to take care of e-mail so quickly, so reflexively, that they don't give enough thought to what they are writing. That is often the worst course of action, especially if anger or emotions are involved. If you yourself receive an e-mail that upsets or outrages you, wait before responding.

It's important to talk like you would if the person was right there. Say hello and say good-bye in a nice way. Show respect by answering e-mails and answering them in a kind manner. When you return an e-mail right away, the recipient knows that you care.

This is a great thing to do for both personal and work e-mails.

The next time you are about to send an important e-mail or letter, try this: As you are about to hit the "Send" button or put the letter into the mailbox, stop for a moment. After the e-mail or letter is on its way, pause again and turn your attention inside. Offer your gratitude in spirit. What's done is done. You can certainly take this lesson and extend it to what you write in blogs and on other Internet sites.

Empathy

A person who makes noise while others are trying to sleep or who swears in front of children is doing so because he is not being empathetic and perceiving the needs and well-being of others.

Empathy is one of the best ways of improving relationships and life in general. Aim to be constructive, positive, and empathetic in your speech. Give support and encouragement. Be open and sensitive to what others are experiencing and you will truly see and hear them. Empathy doesn't only resolve problems; it also makes us feel better, healthier, more satisfied, and more creative. In allowing you to identify with another person for the sake of understanding her, empathy brings relief and contentment to that person and to you.

When someone is in distress, that is when she needs a listener who is understanding and compassionate. Removing judgment, comparison, competition, and so on from your communication will make you immediately able to resonate or be empathetic. It is freeing and opening to you and those you communicate with. And just being considerate is another display of empathy. So tiptoe when someone is sleeping and don't swear, especially around children.

Encouragement

In order to build more satisfying relationships with the people around you, make a conscious effort to express more affirmation and encouragement. It is always better to say something kind or encouraging than to speak sharply or derisively. Use your words to encourage others.

Encouragement is an attempt to notice others' strengths, acknowledge their efforts, and communicate to them that they can succeed. Helping people know and feel that what they do matters will help you have a more positive relationship with them.

Encouragement and praise not only produce good feelings, they also help every person learn and grow. When people feel valued, when their efforts are noticed and encouraged, they are more likely to make an effort to repeat the good behavior or new skill.

Offering encouragement takes extra effort and a sense of purpose. It doesn't happen accidentally. Be especially attentive to the needs of others. Don't just say, "Good job!" Provide details, especially concerning progress. Showing someone that you're paying attention can be encouraging in itself. Offer suggestions, and remember that constructive criticism can be as inspiring as compliments. Use your imagination when giving feedback or support.

Family

We all fall into the trap of taking family members for granted, of treating them with less care because we are so used to being around them—and yet that is an odd thing, that we treat strangers better than our loved ones at times. The quality of our communications with family members should be extremely high because we value them; they either gave birth to us or are close relatives, or we gave birth to them.

We can be mindful of what we are doing when we speak to our family. We can also be mindful in listening. Instead of commenting on what others do or criticizing them, practice speaking only what is true and useful, kind and wise, appropriate and timely. To be kind and honest with family members makes your mind quieter and more open, your heart happier and more peaceful.

Speech is one area in which karma, where every action has a result, can be seen having a direct effect. Notice the intentions that motivate your speech to family. Direct your attention to the state of mind that precedes talking, the motivation for your comments, observations, responses, and questions. What is influencing what you say to your various family members?

After looking at the motivation for your speech, notice its effects. In discovering the power of your words, you can practice using Right Speech to cultivate more happiness in your family.

Forgiveness

Forgiveness is at the heart of all happiness. Forgiveness is an exercise that involves letting go of your anger, bitterness, and blame toward a person who has hurt or wronged you (or who you believe has done this). Whether these are big or small matters, they are real to us and negatively affect us. Often, the person who committed the wrong is not even aware that he did something hurtful.

Speaking forgiveness or writing a forgiveness letter may go over what happened, or what you wish the other person had done or said instead, but it ends with an explicit statement of forgiveness and understanding. You are unburdened by the process and now can move forward.

This may be hard to do if you view the act as unforgivable and you feel too overwhelmed by negative feelings to start letting it go. If that is true, just try. Maybe you just put it in a letter and wait to send it or wait to deliver the message in person. You might have to set it aside and come back to it at a later time. Forgiveness takes effort, motivation, and willpower. Weigh the advantages of forgiveness and resentment—then choose.

Friends

Friendship is the most beautiful, most powerful, and most valuable treasure in life. If you always remain sincere in your interactions with others, you will one day naturally come to find yourself surrounded by good friends.

It's important to understand that friendship depends on *you*, not on the other person. It all comes down to your own attitude and contribution. You can enrich the time shared with your friends by being attentive, loving, open, and sympathetic. Become the kind of person who sticks by her friends with unchanging loyalty through thick and thin.

Be friendly to the people around you. Being kind is uncomplicated. You can practice this any time, anywhere, with anyone. If you consistently cultivate generosity and loving-kindness to all, you'll make lots of friends, many will love you, and you'll feel relaxed and peaceful. When you love and accept others as they are, you will have friends everywhere.

Getting to Know Someone

Put your best self out there, be sincere, and be in the present moment. Listen to those you are trying to get to know. The best way to make them understand your interest is to listen to them. You can ask thousands of questions, but you have to listen for the answers. Those who take their time getting to know people generally end up with better relationships.

For your part, *don't overshare*. People feel uncomfortable when they hear the deepest secrets of someone they don't know well. And not oversharing also means not gossiping about others, which you may do to put yourself in a better light. Well, it doesn't work that way. If you disparage another person, it really just makes you look bad. Put yourself in the other person's shoes when communicating.

You can see that getting to know someone is mostly about speech. Right Speech—being truthful and kind, not gossiping or commenting about others, not swearing or using other divisive speech, and attentive listening—is your most important tool. It is also essential that you not compare the person to people you have had as friends or have dated in the past; stay in the moment with this new acquaintance. And when you are talking to this person, don't start planning your future with her in your head; again, stay in the present moment. Take your time and enjoy getting to know each other.

Gratitude and Appreciation

A great way to promote gratitude and appreciation in your life is to write it down. You can write about "things to be happy about," "things to be grateful for," or "things I appreciate." Whatever you call it and in whatever way you choose to write these things down, this type of inner exploration can help you become happier and more content.

Gratitude is essential to transform your path to happiness. It is important to give thanks each day for the abundance that exists in your life. The more you are grateful, the more you will have to be grateful about. It's really simple, and a process that feeds itself. It teaches you to pay attention, to be awake in the present moment, to be grateful for the little things in everyday life.

You could start by writing down, every evening, five things from the day that you are grateful about. Sometimes you will have amazing things to be grateful for and other times you may struggle to find the five things and start writing entries that seem very simplistic to you.

Another great practice is telling people that you are grateful for them in your life, for what they have done, for who they are. Telling a stranger who has given you something—directions, good service, a smile—that you are grateful for what he has done and given you is another form of connection. Spread the idea of gratitude through your speech and writing.

Humility

"Lighten up" is a pretty good reminder when you take so many things too seriously, when you get angry about petty matters, or when you spend time thinking and worrying about yourself. If you have a different opinion from someone, it is probably not imperative that the other person understand your point of view. And explaining it, no matter how many times, will not necessarily change that person's mind. Accepting this is part of the definition of humility.

Think about this: most things don't amount to anything worth getting really upset about. If you take a circumstance that is upsetting and ask yourself if it will matter (or if you will even remember it) in a day, a week, a month, a year, or ten years—well, you know that the majority of the time the answer will be "no," that it will not matter. Yesterday you worried about wearing the right outfit today. But tomorrow when someone asks you what you wore the day before, you most likely won't remember what the outfit was! We each have times when we get in a tizzy about something, when what we would most benefit from is letting it go and lightening up.

Your example of "lightening up" will not go unnoticed by family, friends, and coworkers. You will have a tremendous positive impact on all those around you.

Humor

Humor can deepen your practice of Right Speech. Humor helps you take a gentler look at things. The humorous view encourages a softening, which can help free us from our masks and puffery. If we can allow it, humor helps remind us that when it comes down to it, there really isn't anyone "there" to be embarrassed, hurt, or humiliated—so let them laugh! Always look for the humor in your situation. Unless we learn to laugh at ourselves, we will never be completely without delusion.

The idea isn't to use humor as another way of hiding, or to be glib about a difficult situation; you can use humor from a place of bravery, to bring attention to the possibility that there's another way of seeing things. Employing a little lightness can bring some relief. You might then be able to relax and try to work with what's present without experiencing it in such a heavy way.

There is a big difference between humor that celebrates and humor that denigrates. We need irreverent humor to undercut self-importance, but we should not poke fun at others (or ourselves) in a personal, hurtful way. There is immense aggression in that; such humor is crude and resentful. But genuine humor is delightful. And laughter can be a bond between people, and puncture pretensions you detect in your own attitudes or behavior.

Instructions

Instructions are needed and used for so many everyday activities: how to type, how to use a computer, how to make a cup of coffee, how to brush your teeth, even how to read for comprehension. Now take this process one step further and practice being specific about instructions you are called upon to give. You can see that offering clear instructions is really important to those you deal with at work, school, and home.

Being specific about what you really want and need is important, just like buying the right ingredients for the dish you plan to make for dinner or ordering the right size of sheets for the bed. It takes courage and patience to be specific about help you need in the kitchen or at the office. Explaining a process or items you need should be done kindly. You may know exactly what needs to be done, but you should not assume the other person has that same knowledge or awareness.

If you want to be unhappy, you let your teenager go out and say, "Be home early." Or you say to the haircutter, "Cut a little off." If you want to be happy, you say what time your teenager is supposed to be home and exactly how much the haircutter should trim. Maybe there are things that don't matter to you, but in most cases you do know what you want and you need to take responsibility for saying what it is. By being specific in this way, you also take pressure off the people you are interacting with. They cannot read your mind and it is unfair for us to assume that they can. When they know exactly what you mean, then they can behave or perform a task in an appropriate manner.

Intention

Right Speech is asking yourself, before you speak: Is it true? Is it kind? Is it beneficial? Does it harm anyone? Is this the right time to say anything? Does what you are about to say improve upon silence?

After discovering what intention is present as you speak, notice the effect of the speech. What response does it get? With the law of karma—that every cause has an effect—we have a choice in each new moment of what response our heart and mind will bring to the situation. In discovering the power of your inner state to determine your speech, you will be able to follow a path that can lead to genuine happiness.

If you behave in ways that cause you shame or leave you feeling anxious, disconnected, or empty, you can use a simple way to reconnect with a more appreciative and loving self. Stop and ask yourself, Is this kind? When the answer is no, you must take definitive action. If you stay mindfully aware of every intention, you will remember to be extra careful of what you say when you are vulnerable or imbalanced.

Internal Talk

That running commentary in your head is something you can do without. You go over things that were said in the past and rehearse things you want to say in the future. The running commentary goes on, and we hope that words in our heads will create the reality we want. But we are not our thoughts, and finding a way to deal with your internal dialogue is necessary to bring you some peace.

Part of why some people are afraid of silence is because then they are faced with the incessant chatter of their minds, which often is about worries, rehashing, planning, daydreaming. Instead of avoiding this by talking or watching television or other mindless activities, why not try meditation? Meditation can help you find a way to see and let go of the thoughts and find calmness in quiet moments.

Very rarely do we stop doing things, be quiet, and pay attention. Meditation can help you create a mental "Off" button. The "Off" button brings peace and quiet. Aim to learn a natural quietness of mind and openness of heart. The quieter you become, the more you can hear.

Stop from time to time during the day and pay attention to that inner dialogue. You are *not* your thoughts, and you need to train yourself *not* to believe the messages your thoughts give. When you are in the midst of a dialogue with yourself, become aware and say to yourself, "Stop talking." When you stop, note what the voices in your head were jabbering about. What are the themes? What is the emotional tone? Watch for when the talking starts again, like a tennis player watches for the ball. Remember, you are not your thoughts and you do not have to believe the messages they impart.

Internet

The strange thing about the Internet is that its inception has improved world communications a hundred times over, yet we're beginning to falter in our real-life relationships. When our social skills go out the window, it may be time to consider taking a break from the Internet. How many times do you see everyone at a restaurant table or in an airport staring at a screen instead of talking to each other or just being together?

Take a short refuge in the inner calm and peace of the quiet mind. Sit still at your desk and do absolutely nothing for two minutes. Can you make it all the way to two minutes? Keep still. By taking a break from the Internet and the computer, you will give your body and mind some time to recuperate and realign—that is, as long as you don't replace the Internet with television or something similar.

Irritation, Frustration, Annoyance

The seeds of full-blown anger are annoyance, frustration, and irritation. Instead of letting anger grow, you can accept such instances with humor, calm serenity, sad serenity, or constructive efforts to improve the situation. When you realize that you are irritated, try putting a little half-smile on your face. Every time you start to smile away your irritation or frustration, you achieve a victory for yourself and those around you.

You might still be irritated, but you will not lose yourself to anger as long as you can tolerate the irritation, be patient, refrain from reacting, and even forgive the injury. Life's tiny troubles—like not having a perfect view at the theater, noticing a new scratch on your car, or just missing a train—don't threaten you in any way. Rise above them. Don't dramatize superficial irritations: it makes them more powerful as hazards to your peace of mind. Why waste energy being irritated by things you can't control?

Turn a source of irritation into an opportunity to be mindful. If you know someone who has the knack of irritating you, try to overlook this unfortunate trait and look at the person from another angle. And avoid situations that provoke you to aggressive reactions. If you see something on television or hear something on the radio that irritates you—change the channel, mute the sound, turn it off. If your irritation remains, you can step back and get a perspective on it. "Wow, I'm really feeling irritated. I think I'll let that go for now so I can concentrate on something nicer."

Kindness

Kindness is a simple but profound concept. The practice of kindness will not only lead to your own individual happiness and the happiness of those around you, but will guide you in a world that is becoming increasingly anxious, cold, difficult, and frightening.

Kindness in speech can be the starting point, the fount from which flow so many other positive qualities, such as generosity, honesty, and patience. You start by being kind to yourself. When you go to bed at night, don't lie there and criticize yourself for something you said or did or something you failed to say or do. Rather, be kind to yourself and grateful for your positive points.

With others, listen more than you talk. Try not to comment on everything others say or do. Would you want them to do that to you? Commenting is just criticism. If what someone is saying or doing is directly affecting you, then pause and consider the most kind way of addressing them or the situation.

Listening

We seem to crave talking and can't get enough of it. In many cases we talk just to hear ourselves speak. Shouldn't we do an equal amount of listening and also seek more silence? The ability to speak, hear, and write languages is unique to humans and we can cultivate these miraculous skills in much more mindful ways.

Our brains pick up all types of information, even from nonverbal clues. But a major portion of what we think we just heard is the product of our imagination. Without realizing it, we fill in the gaps in other people's utterances, recreating others' speech as they are offering it. But in doing this, we are not really listening.

When practicing mindful listening, give others your full attention. Let yourself open up to the words that are coming toward you. Concentrate on every word the other person says. Try to understand the meaning of the words that are being spoken. And remember that the more you listen to others, the more they will listen to you.

Remember, too, that silence is golden. Not bragging or seeking recognition will ensure that you do not become complacent, and will endear you to everyone. Not saying anything when you have nothing useful and kind to say will prove you wise.

Meetings

Meetings involve communication among a group, or at least between two people, so Right Speech is a major factor in whether a meeting is a positive or negative experience.

One way to approach meetings is to practice two or three minutes of mindful meditation before the meeting, or at least take a moment to pause before entering the room. If you go to a lot of meetings, you can make a card that says "Breathe" and put it somewhere where you can see it.

As you enter a meeting, keep an open mind and practice patience. Be where you are, wait your turn, and contribute. Every meeting offers a unique chance for enlightenment.

Depending on the company or organization having the meeting, instead of jumping straight into the meeting, the leader can ask the group to start with a pause. This instantly makes everyone more aware of what's in the present moment. Just this awareness can make a big difference.

You can also meditate on the meeting while you are in it. Make it your object of awareness. Open yourself fully to the experience. If you find yourself drifting off, inattentive, or bored, simply note those feelings and bring your attention back to your object of awareness. If you are called upon to speak, pause for a long breath before responding.

Neighbors

Sharing small talk or gardening lore is a way in which neighbors can benefit from a shared fence over which they can speak to each other. Value such occasions—and make the most of them. Be a good listener with neighbors when you meet up.

Neighbors can be more helpful than friends or relatives in some ways, simply because they live so close by.

But what if there are issues you have to deal with, like noise? You can try to talk to your neighbors calmly and kindly. Perhaps they have no idea you can hear their noise or that you have children or pets affected by the noise.

If you are having trouble resolving this issue with the neighbor's cooperation, you might do well to accept the noise as part of your meditation practice. Stay loosely focused on your breathing and let the noise be a sort of secondary focus of the practice. If you stop seeing the noise as the enemy and instead see it as part of your practice, then you will likely see the conflict diminish.

Overthinking

Thinking and ruminations can be very compelling. You believe that if you think about something enough, you will be able to figure things out. But overthinking causes stress and insecurity to escalate.

Free yourself as soon as you recognize you are overthinking. Distract yourself with an activity engrossing enough that you can't lapse back into rumination. That usually means doing an activity that makes you feel amused, curious, happy, or peaceful.

When you note overthinking, you can pause. Another strategy is to set aside a "thinking time" or a journaling time each day to pour out the thoughts and then let them go. The important thing is the practice in recognizing that you are overthinking.

Learn how to avoid future overthinking traps. If certain people, places, situations, and times trigger your overthinking—then you can avoid or modify these triggers. Above all, meditation is practice in recognizing and letting go of overthinking and rumination.

Patience

For mindful communication, you need patience. Patience is the foundation of discovering simplicity and it is a gesture of profound kindness. Patience is motivated by a desire for inward and outward peace and by faith in your ability to accept things as they are. Patience is about overcoming anger and aggression. Patience means buying time with mindfulness so that you can use Right Speech.

Because patience helps enlarge your perspective beyond identifying with thoughts and opinions, you are less likely to speak from a tight, self-protected space and you are more able to put yourself in someone else's shoes.

Patience in the face of anger is one of the hardest practices. It's all too easy to lose your patience with people and speak or write unkindly. A wise person knows that showing kindness and compassion is the most effective way to bring out the best in others. It means taking a few deep breaths instead of yelling in frustration. It means pausing to try to understand someone before responding. When someone ridicules or insults you, you should not retaliate by returning the sarcasm and slander, but practice patience instead.

Pets

Your pets can't talk back. They offer you love and surely you offer them love, too. But they can be frustrating, as when you need your dog to do his business when you have to get to work and he is out there in the freezing cold enjoying nature—not the least bit interested in complying with your plea.

Remember to be kind in communicating with your furry friends. They mess up sometimes, get into mischief, and don't cooperate. You can't communicate with them using words they understand, but they can understand the tone of those words. It's okay to be firm and try to get them to behave with repeated, calm commands. But they are animals with animal instincts and behaviors living in the alien world of humans. Be as kind as you can be in speaking to them.

Public Places

Because we witness so much rude talk in movies and television shows and social media venues, this often rolls over into how we speak to others in public. In general, people nowadays seem less concerned with what they say, even when it is overheard by strangers in public places. They snap at their partner, they talk on a Bluetooth device in the middle of a store, they swear at something or someone even when children are present. There's a lot of wrong speech going on in public places.

Set a good example for others by being mindful of your speech. If you don't have something nice to say, don't say anything at all. Most of the time, wrong speech in public is also unnecessary speech. If your partner tries to buy something silly at a store, do you really need to denigrate him or her? Kindly discuss the matter. When someone brushes past you, don't mutter something nasty at them. Are you trying to get into a brouhaha?

Avoid talking about personal problems in a public place. Talking about personal problems in a public place can make those around you feel highly uncomfortable and can be embarrassing for you. Make sure you save these conversations for home or another private place. Practice Right Speech in public places. Say only what is necessary, useful, and kind.

Reacting and Responding

Most of our problems are created by our own reactions. Absurdly, we blame the person who triggered the anger or sadness. It's difficult to get angry or sad unless it is a tendency inside us waiting to be triggered. You can control your own reaction to the circumstances in your life.

How can you learn to witness situations you cannot change rather than react to them? Become aware of the constant stream of judging and reacting in inner and outer experiences that you can get caught up in and learn to step back from it. You can keep quiet long enough to respond rather than react.

If you engage in harsh, abusive, or sarcastic speech, you do not invite another to trust or listen to what you are trying to say. And if someone shows anger toward you, you should not react with anger. It's more productive and a lot more fun to respond creatively than to react cantankerously.

Practice being aware of what's happening in the present moment without reacting. Take several deep breaths, creating space between the stimulus and the reaction. From a peaceful center you can respond instead of react. Happiness is not about what happens to you, but how you choose to respond to what happens.

Reading

Life has much to do with verbalization—talking, thinking, reading, writing. We worship language and are addicted to it. Pay attention to what you are feeding your mind. When you read something, it is as if the story happened to you. Be conscious of what you read and feed your mind. Read widely, think deeply, and retain your sense of discrimination.

Reading is a great refuge. It can take you anywhere in the world. It can let you feel all of the human emotions. It inserts ideas and knowledge in your head. There are lots of times when you read something that transports you, that makes you feel warm and fuzzy inside, that inspires you and gets your creative juices flowing.

In reading, whenever you come across something you want to remember, reread it a few times, let it sink in, savor it. After reading it, close your eyes and pay attention to your breathing for a minute. That will let the learning settle into your mind and body.

Be aware while reading. Read slowly and calmly so that the very act of reading is peace. Read uplifting words, especially before going to sleep.

Relatives

Be aware of the suffering caused by unmindful speech and the inability to listen to family members. Practice cultivating loving speech and deep listening in order to bring joy and happiness to others and relieve them of their suffering. Knowing that words can create happiness or suffering, you learn to speak truthfully, with language that inspires self-confidence, joy, and hope. Be determined not to gossip or criticize or condemn. Refrain from uttering words that can cause division or discord. And make the effort to reconcile and resolve all conflicts, however small.

We all know about the holidays or other social situations, when even the calmest people can get frazzled, and situations where difficult relatives are present. Don't just react in the moment; consider how you want to act. Don't bite bait for an argument or to enter into gossiping or criticizing others. You don't have to engage. If you have a strong negative opinion, keep it to yourself. There are many times when walking away is the best choice.

At family events and on holidays, some people eat and drink too much as a reaction to the stress. This can lead to unmindful speech, so think about what you are doing. You might think you are making a joke, but it may not be funny at all if you are poking fun at a personal foible or gaffe made by someone. Mouths start flapping in situations where people are nervous, stressed, uncomfortable, or feeling tipsy. It takes a lot of practice to use Right Speech in these situations, but everyone benefits if you do.

Silence and Quiet

Learn to tolerate silence. Do not let it intimidate you. Embrace it. Listen instead. Relax to the quiet that contains the mind. In a world full of noise, silence can be a scary thing. But when you embrace silence, it becomes a friend. It becomes an important part of your life because it enables you to focus on the present. Don't become nervous about the absence of speech; allow yourself and others to be silent.

Give yourself some silent time each day, for in moments of emptiness the spirit enters. Float in the emptiness of the silence. Let it fill your body and mind.

A silent lunch break can go a long way in helping you get in touch with inner peace. By maintaining silence, you are less distracted and can be more fully aware of such things as how quickly you eat, how well you chew your food, what food you desire, and how much you eat.

Imagine yourself sitting in a very quiet place. You attempt to speak words of wisdom but they will not come out. Each time the words will not come out, you gain energy in your spirit. You feel the wisdom building up inside you. You are learning the wisdom of silence. You stop trying to speak and you just sit, becoming wiser. Capable of practicing silence, you are free as a bird, in touch with the essence of things. Silence is a time for looking deeply.

Before you speak, be silent for a moment. Allow the right words to form. Expressing yourself clearly will also improve the answers you receive. If you cannot say something useful, you should keep Noble Silence.

Social Media

In this age of social media, texting, e-mail, and information overload, how do we keep the precepts of Right Speech? With social media as a global communication tool, there are many examples of speech used to divisively separate people. Comments and tweets that are negative tend to outweigh speech that leads to peace and harmony. In this era, Right Speech is of utmost importance in helping us to use social media as a tool to promote peace and harmony.

There is a lot of egoistic chatter that goes on in social networking sites. However, there are also a lot of topics or situations where skillful, right-minded responses can be of benefit to others.

Here are some questions to ask yourself before you communicate on the Internet:

- ✸ Is this the right time to speak or write?

- ✸ Am I speaking truthfully?

- ✸ Am I speaking kindly and gently?

- ✸ Is what I am about to say useful or helpful?

Put another way:

- ✸ Do not tell lies or deceive.

- ✸ Do not slander others or speak in a way that causes disharmony.

- ✸ Abstain from rude, impolite, or abusive language.

- ✸ Do not indulge in idle talk or gossip.

Solitude

In our society there is a general loss of solitude and, at the same time, a hunger for it. Mental solitude (Noble Silence) is a way to empty, cleanse, heal, and renew the heart and mind. The two types of solitude, bodily solitude and mental solitude, should be cultivated. Sometimes it is easy to find time for solitude, but even when it is difficult to find some alone time, you can make an effort.

We should spend some time by ourselves, in bodily solitude. We need to be alone in order to have a chance to gain mental stillness. Mental solitude means being alert and aware. Being alone—not reading or watching television or listening to music or even thinking—is productive for your spirit. In solitude we gain peace and balance, like the wind not caught by any net.

Wake up a half hour before everyone else or take a few minutes after everyone leaves for work or school or after others go to bed.

You can take your lunch hour alone. Taking a walk or hike by yourself is also a good way to find solitude. Even staying in bed all of a weekend morning can do the trick. Use times like these for your renewal.

Strangers

Civility toward strangers is an old-fashioned virtue, implying well-mannered consideration for all around you. If you value this quality and observe its simple precepts, you'll make people feel better about life. The effort involved is not great. Keep your poise and your patience. Be gracious with all.

Occasionally in our everyday life we'll receive from a stranger a smile that surprises us by its openness and generosity—as if from a heart overflowing with goodwill. Value such smiles as precious gifts—and return them. Smiles bring the beauty of a giving heart to a giving face.

Around a stranger, start by saying hello. Don't expect any outcome; don't be offended or disappointed if someone does not respond to you. Tolerate rejection; it isn't about you—it's about where that person is at mentally. And do not mind what strangers think. That does not mean you should be rude, crude, and obscene.

It means that you should not worry about what strangers think about your talking to them. It should not test your courage or make you afraid to talk to someone you do not yet know.

Imagine that a stranger is already your friend and you will speak nicely to her. Smile and laugh; it's contagious!

Suffering and Pain

All the happiness in the world comes from thinking of others; all the suffering in the world comes from thinking only of oneself. Remember this before you communicate in speech or writing.

Do not think that because you are suffering you can speak harshly, retaliate, or punish others. Breathe in and remember that harsh or angry speech causes more suffering for you as well as for others. Right Speech displays your capacity for calm and compassion.

You know that if a person speaks with an impure mind, suffering follows. If a person speaks with a pure mind, joy follows. Words can cause suffering, so vow to speak only with kindness and love. Listen deeply. Never speak words that could cause division and discord. Work to avoid or resolve conflict. Remember, only unhappy people act in a nasty way. Have some compassion for their suffering.

Commit to cultivating loving speech and deep listening in order to bring joy and happiness to others and relieve others of their suffering. Learn to speak truthfully, with words that inspire self-confidence, joy, and hope. Be determined not to gossip, criticize, or condemn. Refrain from uttering words that can cause division or discord. Make efforts to reconcile and resolve all conflicts, however small.

Sympathy

The goal of expressing sympathy is to offer your compassion and concern. Compassion is active sympathy. The ideal is to selflessly act to alleviate suffering wherever it appears.

The most important thing is to communicate that you care about a person and that you are available as a source of support. Think of a simple and succinct way of communicating your empathy. If you are at a loss for words, tell the person, "I'm sorry for your loss and suffering," and let him know that you care. What you say lets him know that you are aware of the emotional difficulty of his situation and helps him feel less isolated in his experience. Acknowledging pain or grief can be very consoling. Offering to listen makes the person feel cared for and lets him know you are there for him at a painful or stressful time.

Saying something simple and kind, thoughtful and not clichéd, is all you need to do. Maybe just admit that you don't know what to say.

Telephone Calls

Being aware of who is with you and where you are when making or receiving a telephone call is important, as is having an awareness of your volume and tone of voice. Watch your language, especially when others can overhear you. Oblivious to those around them, some cell phone users feel free to pepper their conversation with obscenities. The people nearby may try not to listen, but it's hard to ignore. Swearing is just lazy communicating, anyway, so start practicing its elimination from your vocabulary.

When you are talking on the telephone, stay connected with your breathing and notice how you are affected. If you are on a call that is difficult, tedious, or bothersome, repeat a mantra.

Remember, a cell phone doesn't have to be on all the time and you don't always have to answer it immediately. Learn to use features like silent ring, vibrate, and voicemail to handle the times when your phone would be bothering others if it rang and you answered it.

Instead of being a slave to the telephone, pause for a moment and let it ring one more time. Let the full ring complete itself. Listen to it. Compose yourself. Make the sound of your ringing telephone into a mindfulness bell calling you back to your center and the present moment.

Text Messaging

We live in a digital world where communication is being passed via the written word through many mediums, including texting and instant messaging. Right Speech is very important in a medium where meaning and intent can be lost or misunderstood with a few unskillfully typed words. Often there is not enough context to glean the intent. Texting and messaging allows people to say things that they would never say to someone in person. Typing out words quickly and hitting "Enter" is all too easy, and encourages us to be impulsive.

The next time you're thinking of sending that text message, ask yourself if what you have to say is true or necessary. Does it need to be expressed at all? Is what you are saying a kind thing? Is it the right time? If you go off on someone via text, you're probably going to experience the reverberations of your bad timing. Give it space, then pick up the phone or see whoever you're speaking to in person.

Never send out a text message (or post a reply on a social network or send out an e-mail) while annoyed or irritated. Try not to have an immediate verbal response when someone says something that triggers a quick emotional response. Bite your tongue and step away from the keyboard or keypad!

Thinking

Most people believe that they are their thoughts. An awful thought enters your mind and then you think, Wow, how could I think like that? But you are not your thoughts. And by observing your thoughts, you can become aware of them without becoming identified with and caught up in them. You are not your thoughts and you need to get used to *not* believing the messages they give. Thinking is all about words, so it is a major part of Right Speech because it drives what comes out of your mouth.

Stop at times and pay attention to your inner dialogue. Watch the thoughts like a tennis player watches the ball. When you observe your thoughts, you learn how to separate yourself from them and not get embroiled in them. They are not who you are. It is extremely useful to distance yourself from thoughts that are feeding anxiety and negative emotions.

Meditation can really help you deal with inner dialogue. Sit and let your thoughts flow by. Don't stop them, but also don't hold on to them. Observe them as you do passing clouds, far off and inevitable. Be indifferent, like the sky. That is all. See thoughts and sensations, but do not judge or hold them. You will feel like you are becoming more like the clear sky or a still pond.

Timing

We each have experienced being in the right place and time for an opportunity, or telling a joke perfectly to the right audience at the right time. Timing means knowing yourself and understanding those around you. Especially when trying to have a talk with someone, asking someone to either listen deeply or bare her soul, timing is crucial.

Timing takes work. Whether you're speaking with a child, partner, friend, parent, boss, or coworker, you can study another person's patterns and rhythms when it comes to talking and listening. Many parents value car rides for the time it allows them to talk with their children. Some couples need time alone to talk productively; others do best if they talk in a crowded restaurant.

Timing also takes understanding. Trying to force someone to talk or listen never works. When the timing is wrong, it adds to stress and does not resolve problems. Trying to get someone to apologize or be sorry never works, either. They are either sorry or not. You can't control that.

If a matter is urgent, don't be afraid to convey to the person that you have something important to talk to her about and that you need to schedule time to do this.

The next time you have the urge to interrupt someone in the course of a conversation, pause. Instead, really listen to the complete thought(s) expressed. Don't just wait for him to finish talking so you can interject. Listen.

Truth

Right Speech comes down to two general principles: Is it true? Is it useful? Practicing these principles, you become attuned to the subtleties of truth and falsehood. Are there times when you shade the truth or exaggerate in some way? A voice rooted in wisdom treasures truthfulness, respect, and compassion.

There are three main types of lie: the black lie, which is a downright falsehood motivated by self-interest; the gray lie, which is similar but does no harm to others; and the white lie, which is designed to avoid hurting people's feelings. Those who believe in the importance of truth will allow themselves to tell only the third type of lie, for the sake of others, and then only after careful consideration. Sometimes it's better to be plainly honest.

In certain situations, such as when someone asks you if you like the awful meal he just served you or the hideous outfit she is wearing, it is more kind to tell a polite white lie than to say what you really think. What would saying what you really think accomplish? Is it useful?

Each of us has experienced what happens when we do not communicate the truth or when we have said something that was not true. Language is an instrument for discovering and communicating truths. Respect this ideal and when you are not sure of the truth, do not speak.

Work and Work Relationships

The workplace is a network of cooperative endeavor. We need Right Speech for the people we serve, both bosses and customers, and other people we interact or work with. Work stress can be greatly reduced simply by an intentional commitment to cultivate calmness and awareness in the domain of work and by letting mindfulness guide our actions and responses in that domain.

If you are having trouble with a colleague, find the most kind way of sorting out the situation. When you feel impatient with your work or colleagues, you need to realize that you are resisting how things are. You are wanting things to change and you are fighting the fact that you do not have total control. Practice mindful breathing at these times.

Also take the time to express support for someone else's project or work. Take the time to know and remember the home situations of your closest colleagues and, if appropriate, the details of their family. A friendly working environment can be of great value.

Happiness lies in a constructive job well done. Happiness comes when your work and words are of benefit to yourself and others. Learn to regard work as integral to your spiritual practice and approach work as a way to elevate your spirit.

Writing

One of the most direct means for dealing with the mind is to write in a journal, on your good days and bad days. Once you enter your thoughts, you can choose to leave them there. You have concerns, commentary, criticisms—once on paper, they lose "steam" and importance. You have "said" them, and maybe will see that they are better left there.

By entering thoughts about great things you saw, heard, smelled, touched—people, places, things, and activities you liked—you are creating a treasure trove of stored happiness that you can go back to.

Even writing about something upsetting or traumatic can positively affect your health and well-being. It is a great coping tool to use in times of trouble and confusion. Since this is only for you, you need to be completely honest with yourself. The nature of the writing process helps us understand, come to terms with, and make sense of upset and trauma.

Writing involves recording your thoughts externally, whether on paper or in the computer. This may allow you to unburden yourself by chronicling your emotions, memories, and thoughts—allowing you to move past your troubles. Your coping abilities will naturally increase by this process, as will your ability to use Right Speech.

Meditations for Right Speech

Your mind swings like a monkey from tree to tree, thought to thought. Most people aren't calmly aware like cats. Many of us are more like undomesticated animals, high-strung and easily spooked. Meditation practices help you sit still and explore the territory of your big mind, to find the calm center that exists in you.

It is important to set aside the time and space for practicing sitting meditation, self-reflection, and other contemplative activities to cultivate Right Speech. This is the space in which you can learn to feel the natural tenderness of your heart, to hear yourself think, to open up and experience the beauty and chaos of the world around you. Mindful communication includes learning how to open up all your senses and really listen to yourself, to others, and to the world.

The first step for the following meditations is to invite your body to relax and release into the ground or cushion or chair. Let your hands gently drape one over the other or one on each knee. Think of the head as reaching up like a mountain top, so that your body does not go slack. Breathe normally.

Thinking will start. It is a habit. See each thought as a railroad car rumbling by. You see it, then let it pass out of view. The hardest part will be letting each thought go. But it's important to not hang on to a thought, thinking more about it or judging it. Just let it keep going by.

This is something you'll probably have to start over and over again, even during a five-minute or twenty-minute sitting. That's okay. That's why it is called practice. See every thought or sensation, acknowledge it without getting caught up by it, let it go, and come back to the breath. The true benefit of sitting still is when you can carry over this mindfulness into your other daily activities.

LISTENING MEDITATION 1

Sit comfortably, whatever that is for you. Let your eyes close gently. Invite your body to relax and release into the ground or cushion. Let go and accept the nondoing of meditation. Become sensitive to and listen to your breath. Breathe through your nose. Feel the air as it goes in and out of the nostrils. Feel the rising and falling of the chest and abdomen. Allow your attention to settle where you feel the breath most clearly. Do not control the breath; allow your breath to be as it is. Follow the breath. Be aware of what is present. Do this for five to twenty minutes. As you gently open your eyes, try to carry the momentum of your mindfulness into whatever your next activity may be.

LISTENING MEDITATION 2

When listening to someone, focus on stilling your mind and opening your heart to fully hear the other person. Concentrate so you are undistracted by your own emotions and feelings. Hear the other person with acceptance and compassion.

LISTENING MEDITATION 3

To train in listening, acknowledge that you need more skill in this area. Choose to be open and accepting and mindful. Take time now to sit quietly and listen. Commit to cultivating loving speech and deep listening in order to bring joy and happiness to others and to relieve their suffering.

HEARING MEDITATION

Turn your attention to focusing on hearing the sounds around you. All the sounds, pleasant and unpleasant, are simply sounds arising and passing away. Note what you hear and let it go. You do not need to respond, judge, interpret, name, or stop the sounds. Note changes in the sounds, coming and going. Whether you like or dislike a sound, relax and follow the breath, staying open for the next sound. The breath is your anchor and it should remind you to relax. Just hear and be present.

TONE OF VOICE
MEDITATION

You know that your voice tends to rise when you experience strong emotions. Choose a simple sound to help bring you back to vocal normality. The sound OM is one that will correct high-pitched tones with a more low, resonant voice. Do this by focusing on your breathing. Intone your chosen mantra and repeat it on every exhalation. This will help dissolve your feelings of anxiety.

FORGIVENESS MEDITATIONS

Meditate on forgiveness to yourself. If there are ways you have harmed yourself or not loved yourself or not lived up to your own expectations, this is the time to let go of the unkindness you feel toward yourself. Say, "For all of the ways I have harmed or hurt myself, knowingly or unknowingly, I offer forgiveness." You can do this as part of your daily meditation and let your intention to forgive yourself work over time.

Meditate on forgiveness for those who have hurt or harmed you: "There are many ways I have been wounded, hurt, abused, and abandoned by others in thought, word, or deed, knowingly or unknowingly. In the many ways others have hurt or harmed me, out of fear, pain, confusion, or anger, I see this as their suffering. To the extent I am ready, I offer them forgiveness. I have carried this pain in my heart too long. For this reason, to those who have caused me harm, I offer you my forgiveness."

COMPASSION
MEDITATION

Do a brief meditation for cultivating compassion when you are having difficulty with a friend or loved one. Sit, looking beyond the conflict, and reflect on the fact that this person is a human being like you. This person has the same desire for happiness and well-being, the same fear of suffering, the same need for love. Note how this meditation softens your feelings.

MEDITATION FOR CHANGING NEGATIVE THOUGHTS

For a day, use your willpower to catch every negative thought that passes through your mind. If you are complaining about the weather or you are disturbed or bothered by anything or anyone, catch those negative thoughts. See them, don't judge them, then let them go. Neutralize a negative thought by substituting a positive one for it. Raise yourself up to a higher spiritual perspective by remembering that everything happens for the best. Contemplate, remember, and study spiritual teachings that can help your mind go beyond the temporary situations in which those negative thoughts arise.

MEDITATION FOR CHANGING NEGATIVE MIND STATES

Choose one of the most frequent and difficult mind states that arise in your life, such as annoyance, frustration, or irritation. In your meditation practice, be particularly aware each time this state arises. Watch for it. Note how it begins and what precedes it. Note if there is a particular thought or image that triggers the mind state. Note how long it lasts and when it ends, and what follows it. Sit and be aware of the breath, watching and waiting for the mind state. Allow it to come and observe it like an old friend. This practice will help you in daily life when annoyance, frustration, or irritation arises. You will have trained yourself to handle it with awareness.

Barbara Ann Kipfer, PhD, is a lexicographer who has authored more than fifty books, including *14,000 Things to be Happy About, The Wish List, Instant Karma, 8,789 Words of Wisdom,* and *Self-Meditation*. Barbara has an MPhil and PhD in Linguistics, a PhD in Archaeology, and an MA and PhD in Buddhist Studies.

Foreword writer **Marc Lesser** is the CEO of the Search Inside Yourself Leadership Institute (http://siyli.org). He is author of *Know Yourself, Forget Yourself* and *Less: Accomplishing More by Doing Less*.